Henry J. Fox

Sabbath Psalter

A Selection of Psalms of Public and Family Worship

Henry J. Fox

Sabbath Psalter

A Selection of Psalms of Public and Family Worship

ISBN/EAN: 9783337043223

Printed in Europe, USA, Canada, Australia, Japan

Cover: Foto ©Lupo / pixelio.de

More available books at **www.hansebooks.com**

SABBATH PSALTER:

A SELECTION OF PSALMS

FOR

PUBLIC AND FAMILY WORSHIP.

COMPILED BY

Rev. HENRY J. FOX, A. M.

New York:
PUBLISHED BY CARLTON & PORTER,
200 MULBERRY-STREET.
1865.

Entered according to Act of Congress, in the year 1865, by

CARLTON & PORTER,

in the Clerk's Office of the District Court of the United States for the Southern District of New York.

PREFACE.

This compilation has been made at the suggestion of eminent ministers of the Methodist Episcopal Church, and is designed to assist clergymen and heads of families in an important part of public and social worship.

While it is desirable to avoid the formalism which too often grows out of services exclusively liturgical, it is at the same time desirable that the people should take some public part in divine service. They should at least unite in the singing of hymns, in the repetition of the Lord's Prayer, and in the reading of God's word.

The compiler dares to hope that the day will come when the General Conference of his own Church will adopt the "Psalter" or some other selection, and that thus the public reading of the scriptures by the people will become uniform and universal.

This selection embraces most of the devotional prayers of David, and nearly all the psalms suited for public and social worship. The selections are designed to be read at the opening of public service, or immediately after the first prayer. They are prepared also with reference to the family altar. The manner of using is obvious.

The compiler hopes that he has supplied all that is needed to give to the services of non-liturgical Churches suitable interest and fullness, and that the regular use of the "Psalter" will tend greatly to the edification and comfort of the Church of God.

NEW YORK, *Sept.*, 1865.　　　HENRY J. FOX.

CALENDAR OF SUNDAYS

FOR SEVEN YEARS.

The following table shows the DATE of each Sunday for seven years, beginning with 1866. The left hand column gives the NUMBER of any Sunday, reckoned from the beginning of the year; the right hand column the PAGE on which the appropriate selection is to be found.

Sundays.	1866.	1867.	1868.	1869.	1870.	1871.	1872.	Page.
1	Jan. 7	Jan. 6	Jan. 5	Jan. 3	Jan. 2	Jan. 1	Jan. 7	5
2	" 14	" 13	" 12	" 10	" 9	" 8	" 14	9
3	" 21	" 20	" 19	" 17	" 16	" 15	" 21	13
4	" 28	" 27	" 26	" 24	" 23	" 22	" 28	17
5	Feb. 4	Feb. 3	Feb. 2	" 31	" 30	" 29	Feb. 4	21
6	" 11	" 10	" 9	Feb. 7	Feb. 6	Feb. 5	" 11	26
7	" 18	" 17	" 16	" 14	" 13	" 12	" 18	29
8	" 25	" 24	" 23	" 21	" 20	" 19	" 25	33
9	March 4	March 3	March 1	" 28	" 27	" 26	March 3	38
10	" 11	" 10	" 8	March 7	March 6	March 5	" 10	42
11	" 18	" 17	" 15	" 14	" 13	" 12	" 17	47
12	" 25	" 24	" 22	" 21	" 20	" 19	" 24	51
13	April 1	" 31	" 29	" 28	" 27	" 26	" 31	56
14	" 8	April 7	April 5	April 4	April 3	April 2	April 7	60
15	" 15	" 14	" 12	" 11	" 10	" 9	" 14	64
16	" 22	" 21	" 19	" 18	" 17	" 16	" 21	69
17	" 29	" 28	" 26	" 25	" 24	" 23	" 28	74
18	May 6	May 5	May 3	May 2	May 1	" 30	May 5	79
19	" 13	" 12	" 10	" 9	" 8	May 7	" 12	83
20	" 20	" 19	" 17	" 16	" 15	" 14	" 19	88
21	" 27	" 26	" 24	" 23	" 22	" 21	" 26	92
22	June 3	June 2	" 31	" 30	" 29	" 28	June 2	96
23	" 10	" 9	June 7	June 6	June 5	June 4	" 9	101
24	" 17	" 16	" 14	" 13	" 12	" 11	" 16	105
25	" 24	" 23	" 21	" 20	" 19	" 18	" 23	110
26	July 1	" 30	" 28	" 27	" 26	" 25	" 30	114
27	" 8	July 7	July 5	July 4	July 3	July 2	July 7	119
28	" 15	" 14	" 12	" 11	" 10	" 9	" 14	123
29	" 22	" 21	" 19	" 18	" 17	" 16	" 21	127
30	" 29	" 28	" 26	" 25	" 24	" 23	" 28	131
31	Aug. 5	Aug. 4	Aug. 2	Aug. 1	" 31	" 30	Aug. 4	136
32	" 12	" 11	" 9	" 8	Aug. 7	Aug. 6	" 11	140
33	" 19	" 18	" 16	" 15	" 14	" 13	" 18	144
34	" 26	" 25	" 23	" 22	" 21	" 20	" 25	148
35	Sept. 2	Sept. 1	" 30	" 29	" 28	" 27	Sept. 1	152
36	" 9	" 8	Sept. 6	Sept. 5	Sept. 4	Sept. 3	" 8	157
37	" 16	" 15	" 13	" 12	" 11	" 10	" 15	161
38	" 23	" 22	" 20	" 19	" 18	" 17	" 22	166
39	" 30	" 29	" 27	" 26	" 25	" 24	" 29	170
40	Oct. 7	Oct. 6	Oct. 4	Oct. 3	Oct. 2	Oct. 1	Oct. 6	175
41	" 14	" 13	" 11	" 10	" 9	" 8	" 13	179
42	" 21	" 20	" 18	" 17	" 16	" 15	" 20	184
43	" 28	" 27	" 25	" 24	" 23	" 22	" 27	188
44	Nov. 4	Nov. 3	Nov. 1	" 31	" 30	" 29	Nov. 3	193
45	" 11	" 10	" 8	Nov. 7	Nov. 6	Nov. 5	" 10	197
46	" 18	" 17	" 15	" 14	" 13	" 12	" 17	201
47	" 25	" 24	" 22	" 21	" 20	" 19	" 24	205
48	Dec. 2	Dec. 1	" 29	" 28	" 27	" 26	Dec. 1	209
49	" 9	" 8	Dec. 6	Dec. 5	Dec. 4	Dec. 3	" 8	214
50	" 16	" 15	" 13	" 12	" 11	" 10	" 15	218
51	" 23	" 22	" 20	" 19	" 18	" 17	" 22	223
52	" 30	" 29	" 27	" 26	" 25	" 24	" 29	227

SABBATH PSALTER.

FIRST SABBATH.

Morning.

Minister. HOW amiable *are* thy tabernacles, O LORD of hosts!

People. My soul longeth, yea, even fainteth for the courts of the LORD: my heart and my flesh crieth out for the living God.

M. Yea, the sparrow hath found a house, and the swallow a nest for herself, where she may lay her young, *even* thine altars, O LORD of hosts, my King, and my God.

P. Blessed *are* they that dwell in thy house: they will be still praising thee.

M. Blessed *is* the man whose strength *is* in thee; in whose heart *are* the ways *of them.*

P. Who passing through the valley of Baca make it a well; the rain also filleth the pools.

M. They go from strength to strength, *every one of them* in Zion appeareth before God.

P. The LORD loveth the gates of Zion more than all the dwellings of Jacob.

M. Glorious things are spoken of thee, O city of God.

P. Of Zion it shall be said, This and that man was born in her: and the Highest himself shall establish her.

M. The LORD shall count, when he writeth up the people, *that* this *man* was born there.

P. O LORD God of hosts, hear my prayer: give ear, O God of Jacob.

M. Behold, O God our shield, and look upon the face of thine anointed.

P. For a day in thy courts *is* better

than a thousand. I had rather be a doorkeeper in the house of my God, than to dwell in the tents of wickedness.

M. For the LORD God *is* a sun and shield: the LORD will give grace and glory: no good *thing* will he withhold from them that walk uprightly.

P. O LORD of hosts, blessed *is* the man that trusteth in thee.

Evening.

Minister. O TASTE and see that the LORD *is* good: blessed *is* the man *that* trusteth in him.

People. O fear the LORD, ye his saints: for *there is* no want to them that fear him.

M. The young lions do lack, and suffer hunger: but they that seek the LORD shall not want any good *thing*.

P. Come, ye children, hearken unto me: I will teach you the fear of the LORD.

M. What man *is he that* desireth life, *and* loveth *many* days, that he may see good?

P. Keep thy tongue from evil, and thy lips from speaking guile.

Depart from evil, and do good; seek peace, and pursue it.

M. The eyes of the Lord *are* upon the righteous, and his ears *are open* unto their cry.

P. The face of the Lord *is* against them that do evil, to cut off the remembrance of them from the earth.

M. The righteous cry, and the Lord heareth, and delivereth them out of all their troubles.

P. The Lord *is* nigh unto them that are of a broken heart; and saveth such as be of a contrite spirit.

M. Many *are* the afflictions of the righteous: but the Lord delivereth him out of them all.

P. He keepeth all his bones: not one of them is broken.

M. Evil shall slay the wicked: and they that hate the righteous shall be desolate.

P. The Lord redeemeth the soul of his servants: and none of them that trust in him shall be desolate.

SECOND SABBATH.

Morning.

Minister. UNTO thee, O Lord, do I lift up my soul.

People. O my God, I trust in thee: let me not be ashamed, let not mine enemies triumph over me.

M. Yea, let none that wait on thee be ashamed: let them be ashamed which transgress without cause.

P. Show me thy ways, O Lord; teach me thy paths.

M. Lead me in thy truth, and teach me: for thou *art* the God of my salvation; on thee do I wait all the day.

P. Remember, O LORD, thy tender mercies and thy loving-kindnesses; for they *have been* ever of old.

M. Remember not the sins of my youth, nor my transgressions: according to thy mercy remember thou me for thy goodness' sake, O LORD.

P. Good and upright *is* the LORD: therefore will he teach sinners in the way.

M. The meek will he guide in judgment: and the meek will he teach his way.

P. All the paths of the LORD *are* mercy and truth unto such as keep his covenant and his testimonies.

M. For thy name's sake, O LORD, pardon mine iniquity; for it *is* great.

P. What man *is* he that feareth the LORD? him shall he teach in the way *that* he shall choose.

M. His soul shall dwell at ease; and his seed shall inherit the earth.

P. The secret of the LORD *is* with

them that fear him; and he will show them his covenant.

Evening.

Minister. SING aloud unto God our strength: make a joyful noise unto the God of Jacob.

Take a psalm, and bring hither the timbrel, the pleasant harp with the psaltery.

People. Blow up the trumpet in the moon, in the time appointed, on our solemn feast day.

M. For this *was* a statute for Israel, *and* a law of the God of Jacob.

P. This he ordained in Joseph *for* a testimony, when he went out through the land of Egypt: *where* I heard a language *that* I understood not.

M. I removed his shoulder from the burden: his hands were delivered from the pots.

P. Thou calledst in trouble, and I delivered thee; I answered thee in the secret place of thunder: I proved thee at the waters of Meribah.

M. Hear, O my people, and I will testify unto thee: O Israel, if thou wilt hearken unto me;

There shall no strange god be in thee; neither shalt thou worship any strange god.

P. I *am* the Lord thy God which brought thee out of the land of Egypt: open thy mouth wide, and I will fill it.

M. But my people would not hearken to my voice; and Israel would none of me.

P. So I gave them up unto their own hearts' lust: *and* they walked in their own counsels.

M. Oh that my people had hearkened unto me, *and* Israel had walked in my ways!

P. I should soon have subdued their enemies, and turned my hand against their adversaries.

M. The haters of the Lord should have submitted themselves unto him: but their time should have endured forever.

P. He should have fed them also with the finest of the wheat: and with honey out of the rock should I have satisfied thee.

THIRD SABBATH.

Morning.

Minister. PRAISE ye the Lord. Praise ye the Lord from the heavens: praise him in the heights.

People. Praise ye him, all his angels: praise ye him, all his hosts.

M. Praise ye him, sun and moon: praise him, all ye stars of light.

P. Praise him, ye heavens of heavens, and ye waters that *be* above the heavens.

M. Let them praise the name of the LORD: for he commanded, and they were created.

P. He hath also stablished them forever and ever: he hath made a decree which shall not pass.

M. Praise the LORD from the earth, ye dragons, and all deeps:

P. Fire, and hail; snow, and vapor; stormy wind fulfilling his word:

M. Mountains, and all hills; fruitful trees, and all cedars:

P. Beasts, and all cattle; creeping things, and flying fowl:

M. Kings of the earth, and all people; princes, and all judges of the earth:

P. Both young men, and maidens; old men, and children:

M. Let them praise the name of the LORD: for his name alone is excellent; his glory *is* above the earth and heaven.

P. He also exalteth the horn of his

people, the praise of all his saints; *even* of the children of Israel, a people near unto him. Praise ye the LORD.

Evening.

Minister. O God, the heathen are come into thine inheritance; thy holy temple have they defiled; they have laid Jerusalem on heaps.

People. The dead bodies of thy servants have they given *to be* meat unto the fowls of the heaven, the flesh of thy saints unto the beasts of the earth.

M. Their blood have they shed like water round about Jerusalem; and *there was* none to bury *them.*

P. We are become a reproach to our neighbors, a scorn and derision to them that are round about us.

M. How long, LORD? wilt thou be angry forever? shall thy jealousy burn like fire?

P. Pour out thy wrath upon the

heathen that have not known thee, and upon the kingdoms that have not called upon thy name.

M. For they have devoured Jacob, and laid waste his dwellingplace.

P. Oh remember not against us former iniquities: let thy tender mercies speedily prevent us: for we are brought very low.

M. Help us, O God of our salvation, for the glory of thy name: and deliver us, and purge away our sins, for thy name's sake.

P. Wherefore should the heathen say, Where *is* their God?

M. Let him be known among the heathen in our sight *by* the revenging of the blood of thy servants *which is* shed:

P. Let the sighing of the prisoner come before thee; according to the greatness of thy power preserve thou those that are appointed to die;

M. And render unto our neighbors

sevenfold into their bosom their reproach, wherewith they have reproached thee, O Lord.

P. So we thy people and sheep of thy pasture will give thee thanks forever: we will show forth thy praise to all generations.

FOURTH SABBATH.

Morning.

Minister. PRAISE the LORD, O Jerusalem; praise thy God, O Zion.

People. For he hath strengthened the bars of thy gates; he hath blessed thy children within thee.

M. He maketh peace *in* thy borders, *and* filleth thee with the finest of the wheat.

P. He sendeth forth his commandment *upon* earth: his word runneth very swiftly.

M. He giveth snow like wool: he scattereth the hoar frost like ashes.

P. He casteth forth his ice like morsels: who can stand before his cold?

M. He sendeth out his word, and melteth them: he causeth his wind to blow, *and* the waters flow.

P. Sing unto the Lord with thanksgiving; sing praise upon the harp unto our God:

M. Who covereth the heaven with clouds, who prepareth rain for the earth, who maketh grass to grow upon the mountains.

P. He giveth to the beast his food, *and* to the young ravens which cry.

M. He delighteth not in the strength of the horse: he taketh not pleasure in the legs of a man.

P. The Lord taketh pleasure in them that fear him, in those that hope in his mercy.

M. He showeth his word unto Jacob,

his statutes and his judgments unto Israel.

P. He hath not dealt so with any nation: and *as for his* judgments, they have not known them. Praise ye the LORD.

Evening.

Minister. UNTO thee, O God, do we give thanks, *unto thee* do we give thanks: for *that* thy name *is* near, thy wondrous works declare.

People. When I shall receive the congregation I will judge uprightly.

M. The earth and all the inhabitants thereof are dissolved: I bear up the pillars of it.

P. I said unto the fools, Deal not foolishly; and to the wicked, Lift not up the horn:

M. Lift not up your horn on high: speak *not* with a stiff neck.

P. For promotion *cometh* neither

from the east, nor from the west, nor from the south.

M. But God *is* the judge: he putteth down one, and setteth up another.

P. For in the hand of the LORD *there is* a cup, and the wine is red; it is full of mixture, and he poureth out of the same: but the dregs thereof, all the wicked of the earth shall wring *them* out, *and* drink *them*.

M. But I will declare forever; I will sing praises to the God of Jacob.

P. All the horns of the wicked also will I cut off; *but* the horns of the righteous shall be exalted.

M. The humble shall see *this, and* be glad: and your heart shall live that seek God.

P. For the LORD heareth the poor, and despiseth not his prisoners.

M. Let the heaven and earth praise him, the seas, and every thing that moveth therein.

P. For God will save Zion, and will

build the cities of Judah: that they may dwell there, and have it in possession.

M. The seed also of his servants shall inherit it: and they that love his name shall dwell therein.

FIFTH SABBATH.

Morning.

Minister. PRAISE ye the LORD. Sing unto the LORD a new song, *and* his praise in the congregation of saints.

People. I will extol thee, my God, O King; and I will bless thy name forever and ever.

M. Every day will I bless thee; and I will praise thy name for ever and ever.

P. Great *is* the LORD, and greatly to be praised; and his greatness *is* unsearchable.

One generation shall praise thy works to another, and shall declare thy mighty acts.

M. I will speak of the glorious honor of thy majesty, and of thy wondrous works.

P. And *men* shall speak of the might of thy terrible acts: and I will declare thy greatness.

They shall abundantly utter the memory of thy great goodness, and shall sing of thy righteousness.

M. The LORD *is* gracious, and full of compassion; slow to anger, and of great mercy.

P. The LORD *is* good to all: and his tender mercies *are* over all his works.

M. All thy works shall praise thee, O LORD; and thy saints shall bless thee.

The eyes of all wait upon thee; and thou givest them their meat in due season.

P. Thou openest thine hand, and satisfiest the desire of every living thing.

M. Happy *is he* that *hath* the God of Jacob for his help, whose hope *is* in the LORD his God:

P. Which made heaven, and earth, the sea, and all that therein *is:* which keepeth truth for ever:

M. Which executeth judgment for the oppressed: which giveth food to the hungry. The LORD looseth the prisoners.

P. The LORD shall reign forever, *even* thy God, O Zion, unto all generations. Praise ye the LORD.

Evening.

Minister. THE fool hath said in his heart, *There is* no God. Corrupt are they, and have done abominable iniquity: *there is* none that doeth good.

People. God looked down from heaven upon the children of men, to see if there were *any* that did understand, that did seek God.

M. Every one of them is gone back: they are altogether become filthy; *there is* none that doeth good, no, not one.

P. Have the workers of iniquity no knowledge? who eat up my people *as* they eat bread: they have not called upon God.

M. There were they in great fear, *where* no fear was: for God hath scattered the bones of him that encampeth *against* thee: thou hast put *them* to shame, because God hath despised them.

P. Oh that the salvation of Israel *were come* out of Zion! when God bringeth back the captivity of his people, Jacob shall rejoice, *and* Israel shall be glad.

M. Why boastest thou thyself in mischief, O mighty man? the goodness of God *endureth* continually.

P. Thy tongue deviseth mischiefs; like a sharp razor, working deceitfully

M. Thou lovest evil more than good; *and* lying rather than to speak righteousness.

Thou lovest all devouring words, O *thou* deceitful tongue.

P. God shall likewise destroy thee forever, he shall take thee away, and pluck thee out of *thy* dwellingplace, and root thee out of the land of the living.

M. The righteous also shall see, and fear, and shall laugh at him:

P. Lo, *this is* the man *that* made not God his strength; but trusted in the abundance of his riches, *and* strengthened himself in his wickedness.

M. But I *am* like a green olive-tree in the house of God: I trust in the mercy of God for ever and ever.

P. I will praise thee forever, because thou hast done *it:* and I will wait on thy name; for *it is* good before thy saints.

SIXTH SABBATH.

Morning.

Minister. PRAISE ye the LORD. Praise ye the name of the LORD; praise *him*, O ye servants of the LORD.

People. Ye that stand in the house of the LORD, in the courts of the house of our God,

M. Praise the LORD; for the LORD *is* good: sing praises unto his name; for *it is* pleasant.

P. For the LORD hath chosen Jacob unto himself, *and* Israel for his peculiar treasure.

M. For I know that the LORD *is* great, and *that* our Lord *is* above all gods.

P. Whatsoever the LORD pleased, *that* did he in heaven, and in earth, in the seas, and all deep places.

M. He causeth the vapors to ascend from the ends of the earth; he maketh lightnings for the rain; he bringeth the wind out of his treasuries.

P. The idols of the heathen *are* silver and gold, the work of men's hands.

M. They have mouths, but they speak not; eyes have they, but they see not;

P. They have ears, but they hear not; neither is there *any* breath in their mouths.

M. They that make them are like unto them: *so is* every one that trusteth in them.

P. Bless the LORD, O house of Israel: bless the LORD, O house of Aaron:

M. Bless the LORD, O house of Levi: ye that fear the LORD, bless the LORD.

P. Blessed be the LORD out of Zion, which dwelleth at Jerusalem. Praise ye the LORD.

Evening.

Minister. THE wicked watcheth the righteous, and seeketh to slay him.

People. The Lord will not leave him in his hand, nor condemn him when he is judged.

M. Make a joyful noise unto God, all ye lands:

P. Sing forth the honor of his name: make his praise glorious.

M. Say unto God, How terrible *art thou in* thy works! through the greatness of thy power shall thine enemies submit themselves unto thee.

P. All the earth shall worship thee, and shall sing unto thee; they shall sing *to* thy name.

M. Come and see the works of God: *he is* terrible *in his* doing toward the children of men.

P. He turned the sea into dry *land:* they went through the flood on foot: there did we rejoice in him.

M. He ruleth by his power forever; his eyes behold the nations: let not the rebellious exalt themselves.

P. O bless our God, ye people, and

make the voice of his praise to be heard:

M. Which holdeth our soul in life, and suffereth not our feet to be moved.

P. For thou, O God, hast proved us: thou hast tried us, as silver is tried.

M. Thou broughtest us into the net; thou laidst affliction upon our loins.

P. Thou hast caused men to ride over our heads; we went through fire and through water: but thou broughtest us out into a wealthy *place*.

SEVENTH SABBATH.

Morning.

Minister. TURN us again, O God, and cause thy face to shine; and we shall be saved.

People. O Lord God of hosts, how long wilt thou be angry against the prayer of thy people?

M. Thou feedest them with the bread of tears; and givest them tears to drink in great measure.

Thou makest us a strife unto our neighbors: and our enemies laugh among themselves.

P. Turn us again, O God of hosts, and cause thy face to shine; and we shall be saved.

M. Thou hast brought a vine out of Egypt: thou hast cast out the heathen, and planted it.

Thou preparedst *room* before it, and didst cause it to take deep root, and it filled the land.

P. The hills were covered with the shadow of it, and the boughs thereof *were like* the goodly cedars.

She sent out her boughs unto the sea, and her branches unto the river.

M. Why hast thou *then* broken down

her hedges, so that all they which pass by the way do pluck her?

The boar out of the wood doth waste it, and the wild beast of the field doth devour it.

P. Return, we beseech thee, O God of hosts: look down from heaven, and behold, and visit this vine;

M. And the vineyard which thy right hand hath planted, and the branch *that* thou madest strong for thyself.

It is burned with fire, *it is* cut down: they perish at the rebuke of thy countenance.

P. Let thy hand be upon the man of thy right hand, upon the son of man *whom* thou madest strong for thyself.

M. So will not we go back from thee: quicken us, and we will call upon thy name.

P. Turn us again, O Lord God of hosts, cause thy face to shine; and we shall be saved.

Evening.

Minister. SURELY I will not come into the tabernacle of my house, nor go up into my bed;

People. I will not give sleep to mine eyes, *or* slumber to mine eyelids,

M. Until I find out a place for the LORD, a habitation for the mighty *God* of Jacob.

P. Lo, we heard of it at Ephratah: we found it in the fields of the wood.

M. We will go into his tabernacles: we will worship at his footstool.

P. Arise, O LORD, into thy rest; thou, and the ark of thy strength.

M. Let thy priests be clothed with righteousness; and let thy saints shout for joy.

P. For thy servant David's sake turn not away the face of thine anointed.

M. For the LORD hath chosen Zion; he hath desired *it* for his habitation.

P. This *is* my rest forever: here will I dwell; for I have desired it.

M. I will abundantly bless her provision: I will satisfy her poor with bread.

P. I will also clothe her priests with salvation: and her saints shall shout aloud for joy.

M. There will I make the horn of David to bud: I have ordained a lamp for mine anointed.

P. His enemies will I clothe with shame: but upon himself shall his crown flourish.

EIGHTH SABBATH.

Morning.

Minister. TRULY God *is* good to Israel, *even* to such as are of a clean heart.

People. But as for me, my feet were

almost gone; my steps had well nigh slipped.

For I was envious at the foolish, *when* I saw the prosperity of the wicked.

M. For *there are* no bands in their death: but their strength *is* firm.

They *are* not in trouble *as other* men; neither are they plagued like *other* men.

P. Therefore pride compasseth them about as a chain; violence covereth them *as* a garment.

M. Their eyes stand out with fatness: they have more than heart could wish.

They are corrupt, and speak wickedly *concerning* oppression: they speak loftily.

P. They set their mouth against the heavens, and their tongue walketh through the earth.

M. Therefore his people return hither: and waters of a full *cup* are wrung out to them.

And they say, How doth God know? and is there knowledge in the Most High?

P. Behold, these *are* the ungodly, who prosper in the world; they increase *in* riches.

M. Verily I have cleansed my heart *in* vain, and washed my hands in innocency.

For all the day long have I been plagued, and chastened every morning.

P. If I say, I will speak thus; behold, I should offend *against* the generation of thy children.

M. When I thought to know this, it *was* too painful for me;

Until I went into the sanctuary of God; *then* understood I their end.

P. Surely thou didst set them in slippery places: thou castedst them down into destruction.

As a dream when *one* awaketh; *so*, O Lord, when thou awakest, thou shalt despise their image.

M. Nevertheless I *am* continually with thee : thou hast holden *me* by my right hand.

Thou shalt guide me with thy counsel, and afterward receive me *to* glory.

P. Whom have I in heaven *but thee?* and *there is* none upon earth *that* I desire besides thee.

M. My flesh and my heart faileth: *but* God *is* the strength of my heart, and my portion forever.

Evening.

Minister. GOD *is* our refuge and strength, a very present help in trouble.

People. Therefore will not we fear, though the earth be removed, and though the mountains be carried into the midst of the sea;

M. Though the waters thereof roar *and* be troubled, *though* the mountains shake with the swelling thereof.

P. There is a river, the streams whereof shall make glad the city of God, the holy *place* of the tabernacles of the Most High.

M. God *is* in the midst of her; she shall not be moved: God shall help her, *and that* right early.

P. The heathen raged, the kingdoms were moved: he uttered his voice, the earth melted.

M. The LORD of hosts *is* with us; the God of Jacob *is* our refuge.

P. Come, behold the works of the LORD, what desolations he hath made in the earth.

M. He maketh wars to cease unto the end of the earth; he breaketh the bow, and cutteth the spear in sunder; he burneth the chariot in the fire.

P. Be still, and know that I *am* God: I will be exalted among the heathen, I will be exalted in the earth.

M. The LORD of hosts *is* with us; the God of Jacob *is* our refuge.

P. I said in my haste, I am cut off from before thine eyes: nevertheless thou heardest the voice of my supplications when I cried unto thee.

M. O love the Lord, all ye his saints: *for* the Lord preserveth the faithful, and plentifully rewardeth the proud doer.

P. Be of good courage, and he shall strengthen your heart, all ye that hope in the Lord.

NINTH SABBATH.

Morning.

Minister. I WAS glad when they said unto me, Let us go into the house of the Lord.

People. Our feet shall stand within thy gates, O Jerusalem.

M. Jerusalem is builded as a city that is compact together:

P. Whither the tribes go up, the

tribes of the LORD, unto the testimony of Israel, to give thanks unto the name of the LORD.

M. For there are set thrones of judgment, the thrones of the house of David.

P. Pray for the peace of Jerusalem: they shall prosper that love thee.

M. Peace be within thy walls, *and* prosperity within thy palaces.

P. For my brethren and companions' sakes, I will now say, Peace *be* within thee.

M. Because of the house of the LORD our God I will seek thy good.

P. They that trust in the LORD *shall be* as mount Zion, *which* cannot be removed, *but* abideth forever.

M. As the mountains *are* round about Jerusalem, so the LORD *is* round about his people from henceforth even forever.

P. Blessed *is* every one that feareth the LORD; that walketh in his ways.

M. If I forget thee, O Jerusalem, let my right hand forget *her cunning.*

P. If I do not remember thee, let my tongue cleave to the roof of my mouth; if I prefer not Jerusalem above my chief joy.

Evening.

Minister. GIVE ear to my prayer, O God; and hide not thyself from my supplication.

People. Attend unto me, and hear me: I mourn in my complaint, and make a noise;

M. Because of the voice of the enemy, because of the oppression of the wicked: for they cast iniquity upon me, and in wrath they hate me.

P. My heart is sore pained within me: and the terrors of death are fallen upon me.

M. Fearfulness and trembling are come upon me, and horror hath overwhelmed me.

P. And I said, Oh that I had wings like a dove! *for then* would I fly away, and be at rest.

M. Lo, *then* would I wander far off, *and* remain in the wilderness.

P. I would hasten my escape from the windy storm *and* tempest.

M. As for me, I will call upon God; and the LORD shall save me.

P. Evening, and morning, and at noon, will I pray, and cry aloud: and he shall hear my voice.

M. He hath delivered my soul in peace from the battle *that was* against me: for there were many with me.

P. Cast thy burden upon the LORD, and he shall sustain thee: he shall never suffer the righteous to be moved.

M. But thou, O God, shalt bring them down into the pit of destruction: bloody and deceitful men shall not live out half their days; but I will trust in thee.

P. Though the Lord *be* high, yet hath he respect unto the lowly: but the proud he knoweth afar off.

M. Though I walk in the midst of trouble, thou wilt revive me: thou shalt stretch forth thine hand against the wrath of mine enemies, and thy right hand shall save me.

TENTH SABBATH.

Morning.

Minister. GOD be merciful unto us, and bless us; *and* cause his face to shine upon us.

People. That thy way may be known upon earth, thy saving health among all nations.

M. Let the people praise thee, O God; let all the people praise thee.

P. O let the nations be glad and sing for joy: for thou shalt judge the people righteously, and govern the nations upon earth.

M. Let the people praise thee, O God; let all the people praise thee.

P. Then shall the earth yield her increase; *and* God, *even* our own God, shall bless us.

M. God shall bless us, and all the ends of the earth shall fear him.

P. The fool hath said in his heart, *There is* no God. They are corrupt, they have done abominable works, *there is* none that doeth good.

M. The LORD looked down from heaven upon the children of men, to see if there were any that did understand, *and* seek God.

P. They are all gone aside, they are *all* together become filthy: *there is* none that doeth good, no, not one.

M. Have all the workers of iniquity no knowledge? who eat up my people *as* they eat bread, and call not upon the LORD.

P. There were they in great fear: for God *is* in the generation of the righteous.

M. Ye have shamed the counsel of the poor, because the LORD *is* his refuge.

P. Oh that the salvation of Israel *were come* out of Zion! when the LORD bringeth back the captivity of his people, Jacob shall rejoice, *and* Israel shall be glad.

Evening.

Minister. BOW down thine ear, O LORD, hear me: for I *am* poor and needy.

Preserve my soul; for I *am* holy: O thou my God, save thy servant that trusteth in thee.

People. Be merciful unto me, O LORD: for I cry unto thee daily.

Rejoice the soul of thy servant: for unto thee, O Lord, do I lift up my soul.

M. For thou, LORD, *art* good, and

ready to forgive; and plenteous in mercy unto all them that call upon thee.

P. Give ear, O LORD, unto my prayer; and attend to the voice of my supplications.

M. In the day of my trouble I will call upon thee: for thou wilt answer me.

P. Among the gods *there is* none like unto thee, O Lord; neither *are there any works* like unto thy works.

M. All nations whom thou hast made shall come and worship before thee, O LORD; and shall glorify thy name.

For thou *art* great, and doest wondrous things: thou *art* God alone.

P. Teach me thy way, O LORD; I will walk in thy truth: unite my heart to fear thy name.

M. I will praise thee, O Lord my God, with all my heart: and I will glorify thy name for evermore.

P. For great *is* thy mercy toward me: and thou hast delivered my soul from the lowest hell.

M. O God, the proud are risen against me, and the assemblies of violent *men* have sought after my soul; and have not set thee before them.

P. But thou, O Lord, *art* a God full of compassion, and gracious, longsuffering, and plenteous in mercy and truth.

M. O turn unto me, and have mercy upon me; give thy strength unto thy servant, and save the son of thine handmaid.

P. Show me a token for good; that they which hate me may see *it*, and be ashamed: because thou, Lord, hast holpen me, and comforted me.

ELEVENTH SABBATH.

Morning.

Minister. BLESS ye God in the congregations, *even* the Lord, from the fountain of Israel.

People. Thy God hath commanded thy strength: strengthen, O God, that which thou hast wrought for us.

M. Because of thy temple at Jerusalem shall kings bring presents unto thee.

P. Rebuke the company of spearmen, the multitude of the bulls, with the calves of the people, *till every one* submit himself with pieces of silver: scatter thou the people *that* delight in war.

M. Princes shall come out of Egypt; Ethiopia shall soon stretch out her hands unto God.

P. Sing unto God, ye kingdoms of the earth; O sing praises unto the Lord;

M. To him that rideth upon the heavens of heavens, *which were* of old; lo, he doth send out his voice, *and that* a mighty voice.

P. Ascribe ye strength unto God: his excellency *is* over Israel, and his strength *is* in the clouds.

M. O God, *thou art* terrible out of thy holy places: the God of Israel *is* he that giveth strength and power unto *his* people. Blessed *be* God.

P. He that is our God *is* the God of salvation; and unto God the Lord *belong* the issues from death.

M. But God shall wound the head of his enemies, *and* the hairy scalp of such an one as goeth on still in his trespasses.

P. The Lord said, I will bring again from Bashan; I will bring *my people* again from the depths of the sea:

M. That thy foot may be dipped in the blood of *thine* enemies, *and* the tongue of thy dogs in the same.

P. They have seen thy goings, O God; *even* the goings of my God, my King, in the sanctuary.

M. The singers went before, the players on instruments *followed* after; among *them were* the damsels playing with timbrels.

Evening.

Minister. THE LORD *is* our defence; and the Holy One of Israel *is* our King.

Then thou spakest in vision to thy Holy One, and saidst, I have laid help upon *one that is* mighty; I have exalted *one* chosen out of the people.

People. I have found David my servant; with my holy oil have I anointed him:

With whom my hand shall be established: mine arm also shall strengthen him.

M. The enemy shall not exact upon him; nor the son of wickedness afflict him.

P. And I will beat down his foes before his face, and plague them that hate him.

But my faithfulness and my mercy *shall be* with him: and in my name shall his horn be exalted.

M. I will set his hand also in the sea, and his right hand in the rivers.

P. He shall cry unto me, Thou *art* my Father, my God, and the Rock of my salvation.

Also I will make him *my* firstborn, higher than the kings of the earth.

M. My mercy will I keep for him for evermore, and my covenant shall stand fast with him.

P. His seed also will I make *to endure* forever, and his throne as the days of heaven.

M. If his children forsake my law, and walk not in my judgments;

If they break my statutes, and keep not my commandments;

Then will I visit their transgression

with the rod, and their iniquity with stripes.

P. Nevertheless, my lovingkindness will I not utterly take from him, nor suffer my faithfulness to fail.

M. My covenant will I not break, nor alter the thing *that is* gone out of my lips.

P. Once have I sworn by my holiness that I will not lie unto David.

M. His seed shall endure forever, and his throne as the sun before me.

P. It shall be established forever as the moon, and *as* a faithful witness in heaven.

TWELFTH SABBATH.

Morning.

Minister. THY way, O God, *is* in the sanctuary: who *is so* great a God as *our* God!

People. Thou *art* the God that doest

wonders: thou hast declared thy strength among the people.

M. Thou hast with *thine* arm redeemed thy people, the sons of Jacob and Joseph.

P. The waters saw thee, O God, the waters saw thee; they were afraid: the depths also were troubled.

M. The clouds poured out water: the skies sent out a sound: thine arrows also went abroad.

P. The voice of thy thunder *was* in the heaven; the lightnings lightened the world: the earth trembled and shook.

M. Thy way *is* in the sea, and thy path in the great waters, and thy footsteps are not known.

P. Thou leddest thy people like a flock by the hand of Moses and Aaron.

M. Give ear, O my people, *to* my law: incline your ears to the words of my mouth.

P. I will open my mouth in a parable: I will utter dark sayings of old:

Which we have heard and known, and our fathers have told us.

M. For he established a testimony in Jacob, and appointed a law in Israel, which he commanded our fathers, that they should make them known to their children:

P. That the generation to come might know *them, even* the children *which* should be born; *who* should arise and declare *them* to their children:

M. That they might set their hope in God, and not forget the works of God, but keep his commandments:

P. And might not be as their fathers, a stubborn and rebellious generation; a generation *that* set not their heart aright, and whose spirit was not steadfast with God.

Evening.

Minister. O SING unto the Lord a new song: sing unto the Lord, all the earth.

People. Sing unto the Lord, bless his name; show forth his salvation from day to day.

M. Declare his glory among the heathen, his wonders among all people.

P. For the Lord *is* great, and greatly to be praised: he *is* to be feared above all gods.

M. For all the gods of the nations *are* idols: but the Lord made the heavens.

P. Honor and majesty *are* before him; strength and beauty *are* in his sanctuary.

M. Give unto the Lord, O ye kindreds of the people, give unto the Lord glory and strength.

P. Give unto the Lord the glory *due*

unto his name: bring an offering, and come into his courts.

M. O worship the LORD in the beauty of holiness: fear before him, all the earth.

P. Say among the heathen *that* the LORD reigneth:

M. The world also shall be established that it shall not be moved: he shall judge the people righteously.

P. Let the heavens rejoice, and let the earth be glad; let the sea roar, and the fulness thereof.

M. Let the field be joyful, and all that *is* therein: then shall all the trees of the wood rejoice before the LORD;

P. For he cometh, for he cometh to judge the earth: he shall judge the world with righteousness, and the people with his truth.

THIRTEENTH SABBATH.

Morning.

Minister. THIS *is* the day *which* the LORD hath made; we will rejoice and be glad in it.

People. Save now, I beseech thee, O LORD: O LORD, I beseech thee, send now prosperity.

M. Blessed *be* he that cometh in the name of the LORD: we have blessed you out of the house of the LORD.

P. God *is* the LORD, which hath showed us light: bind the sacrifice with cords, *even* unto the horns of the altar.

M. Thou *art* my God, and I will praise thee: *thou art* my God, I will exalt thee.

P. O give thanks unto the LORD; for *he is* good: for his mercy *endureth* forever.

M. Let Israel now say, that his mercy *endureth* forever.

P. Let the house of Aaron now say, that his mercy *endureth* forever.

M. Let them now that fear the Lord say, that his mercy *endureth* forever.

P. I will praise thee with my whole heart: before the gods will I sing praise unto thee.

M. I will worship toward thy holy temple, and praise thy name for thy lovingkindness and for thy truth: for thou hast magnified thy word above all thy name.

P. In the day when I cried thou answeredst me, *and* strengthenedst me *with* strength in my soul.

M. All the kings of the earth shall praise thee, O Lord, when they hear the words of thy mouth.

P. Yea, they shall sing in the ways of the Lord: for great *is* the glory of the Lord.

Evening.

Minister. I SAID, I will take heed to my ways, that I sin not with my tongue : I will keep my mouth with a bridle, while the wicked is before me.

People. I was dumb with silence; I held my peace, *even* from good; and my sorrow was stirred.

M. My heart was hot within me; while I was musing the fire burned: *then* spake I with my tongue.

P. Be merciful unto me, O God, be merciful unto me : for my soul trusteth in thee : yea, in the shadow of thy wings will I make my refuge, until *these* calamities be overpast.

M. I will cry unto God most high; unto God that performeth *all things* for me.

P. He shall send from heaven, and save me *from* the reproach of him that would swallow me up. God shall send forth his mercy and his truth.

M. My soul *is* among lions : *and* I lie *even among* them that are set on fire, *even* the sons of men, whose teeth *are* spears and arrows, and their tongue a sharp sword.

P. Be thou exalted, O God, above the heavens; *let* thy glory *be* above all the earth.

M. They have prepared a net for my steps; my soul is bowed down: they have digged a pit before me, into the midst whereof they are fallen *themselves.*

P. My heart is fixed, O God, my heart is fixed: I will sing and give praise.

M. Awake up, my glory; awake, psaltery and harp: I *myself* will awake early.

P. I will praise thee, O Lord, among the people: I will sing unto thee among the nations.

M. For thy mercy *is* great unto the heavens, and thy truth unto the clouds.

P. Be thou exalted, O God, above the heavens : *let* thy glory *be* above all the earth.

FOURTEENTH SABBATH.

Morning.

Minister. O CLAP your hands, all ye people; shout unto God with the voice of triumph.

People. For the Lord most high *is* terrible; *he is* a great King over all the earth.

M. He shall subdue the people under us, and the nations under our feet.

P. He shall choose our inheritance for us, the excellency of Jacob whom he loved.

M. God is gone up with a shout, the Lord with the sound of a trumpet.

P. Sing praises to God, sing praises: sing praises unto our King, sing praises.

M. For God *is* the King of all the earth: sing ye praises with understanding.

P. God reigneth over the heathen: God sitteth upon the throne of his holiness.

M. The princes of the people are gathered together, *even* the people of the God of Abraham: for the shields of the earth *belong* unto God: he is greatly exalted.

P. I have seen the wicked in great power, and spreading himself like a green bay tree.

Yet he passed away, and, lo, he *was* not: yea, I sought him, but he could not be found.

M. Mark the perfect *man*, and behold the upright: for the end of *that* man *is* peace.

P. But the transgressors shall be

destroyed together: the end of the wicked shall be cut off.

, *M.* But the salvation of the righteous *is* of the LORD: *he is* their strength in the time of trouble.

P. And the LORD shall help them, and deliver them: he shall deliver them from the wicked, and save them, because they trust in him.

Evening.

Minister. BEHOLD, bless ye the LORD, all *ye* servants of the LORD, which by night stand in the house of the LORD.

People. Lift up your hands *in* the sanctuary, and bless the LORD.

M. The LORD that made heaven and earth bless thee out of Zion.

P. Let my prayer be set forth before thee *as* incense; *and* the lifting up of my hands *as* the evening sacrifice.

M. Set a watch, O LORD, before my mouth; keep the door of my lips.

P. Incline not my heart to *any* evil thing, to practise wicked works with men that work iniquity: and let me not eat of their dainties.

M. Let the righteous smite me; *it shall be* a kindness: and let him reprove me; *it shall be* an excellent oil, *which* shall not break my head: for yet my prayer also *shall be* in their calamities.

P. When their judges are overthrown in stony places, they shall hear my words; for they are sweet.

M. Our bones are scattered at the grave's mouth, as when one cutteth and cleaveth *wood* upon the earth.

P. But mine eyes *are* unto thee, O God the Lord: in thee is my trust; leave not my soul destitute.

M. The Lord *is* righteous: he hath cut asunder the cords of the wicked.

P. Let them all be confounded and turned back that hate Zion.

M. Let them be as the grass *upon*

the housetops, which withereth afore it groweth up:

Wherewith the mower filleth not his hand; nor he that bindeth sheaves his bosom.

P. Neither do they which go by say, The blessing of the LORD *be* upon you: we bless you in the name of the LORD.

FIFTEENTH SABBATH.

Morning.

Minister. GIVE the king thy judgments, O God, and thy righteousness unto the king's son.

He shall judge thy people with righteousness, and thy poor with judgment.

People. The mountains shall bring peace to the people, and the little hills, by righteousness.

M. He shall judge the poor of the people, he shall save the children of the needy, and shall break in pieces the oppressor.

P. They shall fear thee as long as the sun and moon endure, throughout all generations.

He shall come down like rain upon the mown grass: as showers *that* water the earth.

M. In his days shall the righteous flourish; and abundance of peace so long as the moon endureth.

P. He shall have dominion also from sea to sea, and from the river unto the ends of the earth.

They that dwell in the wilderness shall bow before him; and his enemies shall lick the dust.

M. The kings of Tarshish and of the isles shall bring presents: the kings of Sheba and Seba shall offer gifts.

Yea, all kings shall fall down before him: all nations shall serve him.

P. For he shall deliver the needy when he crieth; the poor also, and *him* that hath no helper.

He shall spare the poor and needy, and shall save the souls of the needy.

M. He shall redeem their soul from deceit and violence: and precious shall their blood be in his sight.

P. And he shall live, and to him shall be given of the gold of Sheba: prayer also shall be made for him continually; *and* daily shall he be praised.

M. There shall be a handful of corn in the earth upon the top of the mountains; the fruit thereof shall shake like Lebanon: and *they* of the city shall flourish like grass of the earth.

P. His name shall endure forever: his name shall be continued as long as the sun: and *men* shall be blessed in him: all nations shall call him blessed.

M. Blessed *be* the LORD God, the

God of Israel, who only doeth wondrous things.

P. And blessed *be* his glorious name forever: and let the whole earth be filled *with* his glory. Amen, and Amen.

Evening.

Minister. O GIVE thanks unto the LORD; call upon his name: make known his deeds among the people.

People. Sing unto him, sing psalms unto him: talk ye of all his wondrous works.

M. Glory ye in his holy name: let the heart of them rejoice that seek the LORD.

P. Seek the LORD, and his strength: seek his face evermore.

M. Remember his marvellous works that he hath done; his wonders, and the judgments of his mouth;

P. O ye seed of Abraham his servant, ye children of Jacob his chosen.

M. He *is* the Lord our God: his judgments *are* in all the earth.

He hath remembered his covenant forever, the word *which* he commanded to a thousand generations.

P. Which *covenant* he made with Abraham, and his oath unto Isaac;

M. And confirmed the same unto Jacob for a law, *and* to Israel *for* an everlasting covenant:

Saying, Unto thee will I give the land of Canaan, the lot of your inheritance:

P. When they were *but* a few men in number; yea, very few, and strangers in it.

M. When they went from one nation to another, from *one* kingdom to another people;

He suffered no man to do them wrong: yea, he reproved kings for their sakes;

Saying, Touch not mine anointed, and do my prophets no harm.

P. I will sing unto the LORD as long as I live: I will sing praise to my God while I have my being.

M. My meditation of him shall be sweet: I will be glad in the LORD.

P. Let the sinners be consumed out of the earth, and let the wicked be no more. Bless thou the LORD, O my soul. Praise ye the LORD.

SIXTEENTH SABBATH.

Morning.

Minister. O LORD God of my salvation, I have cried day *and* night before thee:

People. Let my prayer come before thee: incline thine ear unto my cry;

M. For my soul is full of troubles: and my life draweth nigh unto the grave.

P. I am counted with them that go

down into the pit : I am as a man *that hath* no strength :

M. Free among the dead, like the slain that lie in the grave, whom thou rememberest no more : and they are cut off from thy hand.

P. Thou hast laid me in the lowest pit, in darkness, in the deeps.

M. Thy wrath lieth hard upon me, and thou hast afflicted *me* with all thy waves.

P. Thou hast put away mine acquaintance far from me; thou hast made me an abomination unto them : *I am* shut up, and I cannot come forth.

M. Mine eye mourneth by reason of affliction : Lord, I have called daily upon thee, I have stretched out my hands unto thee.

P. Wilt thou show wonders to the dead? shall the dead arise *and* praise thee?

M. Shall thy lovingkindness be declared in the grave? *or* thy faithfulness in destruction?

P. Shall thy wonders be known in the dark? and thy righteousness in the land of forgetfulness?

M. But unto thee have I cried, O Lord; and in the morning shall my prayer prevent thee.

Lord, why castest thou off my soul? *why* hidest thou thy face from me?

P. I *am* afflicted and ready to die from *my* youth up: *while* I suffer thy terrors I am distracted.

M. Thy fierce wrath goeth over me; thy terrors have cut me off.

They came round about me daily like water; they compassed me about together.

P. Lover and friend hast thou put far from me, *and* mine acquaintance into darkness.

Evening.

Minister. BLESSED *is* the man that walketh not in the counsel of the ungodly, nor standeth in the way of sinners, nor sitteth in the seat of the scornful.

People. But his delight *is* in the law of the LORD; and in his law doth he meditate day and night.

M. And he shall be like a tree planted by the rivers of water, that bringeth forth his fruit in his season; his leaf also shall not wither; and whatsoever he doeth shall prosper.

P. The ungodly *are* not so: but *are* like the chaff which the wind driveth away.

M. Therefore the ungodly shall not stand in the judgment, nor sinners in the congregation of the righteous.

P. For the LORD knoweth the way of the righteous: but the way of the ungodly shall perish.

M. Blessed *is he whose* transgression *is* forgiven, *whose* sin *is* covered.

Blessed *is* the man unto whom the LORD imputeth not iniquity, and in whose spirit *there is* no guile.

P. I acknowledged my sin unto thee, and mine iniquity have I not hid. I said, I will confess my transgressions unto the LORD; and thou forgavest the iniquity of my sin.

M. For this shall every one that is godly pray unto thee in a time when thou mayest be found: surely in the floods of great waters they shall not come nigh unto him.

P. Thou *art* my hiding place; thou shalt preserve me from trouble; thou shalt compass me about with songs of deliverance.

M. I will instruct thee, and teach thee in the way which thou shalt go: I will guide thee with mine eye.

P. Be ye not as the horse, *or* as the mule, *which* have no understanding:

whose mouth must be held in with bit and bridle, lest they come near unto thee.

M. Many sorrows *shall be* to the wicked: but he that trusteth in the Lord, mercy shall compass him about.

P. Be glad in the Lord, and rejoice, ye righteous: and shout for joy, all *ye that are* upright in heart.

SEVENTEENTH SABBATH.

Morning.

Minister. OH give thanks unto the Lord; for *he is* good: for his mercy *endureth* forever.

Oh give thanks unto the God of gods: for his mercy *endureth* forever.

People. Oh give thanks to the Lord of lords: for his mercy *endureth* forever.

M. To him who alone doeth great

wonders: for his mercy *endureth* forever.

To him that by wisdom made the heavens: for his mercy *endureth* forever.

P. To him that stretched out the earth above the waters: for his mercy *endureth* forever.

M. To him that made great lights: for his mercy *endureth* forever:

The sun to rule by day: for his mercy *endureth* forever:

P. The moon and stars to rule by night: for his mercy *endureth* forever.

M. To him that smote Egypt in their firstborn: for his mercy *endureth* forever:

And brought out Israel from among them: for his mercy *endureth* forever:

P. With a strong hand, and with a stretched out arm: for his mercy *endureth* forever.

M. To him which divided the Red

sea into parts: for his mercy *endureth* forever:

And made Israel to pass through the midst of it: for his mercy *endureth* forever:

P. But overthrew Pharaoh and his host in the Red sea: for his mercy *endureth* forever.

M. To him which led his people through the wilderness: for his mercy *endureth* forever.

P. Who remembered us in our low estate: for his mercy *endureth* forever.

M. And hath redeemed us from our enemies: for his mercy *endureth* forever.

Who giveth food to all flesh: for his mercy *endureth* forever.

P. O give thanks unto the God of heaven: for his mercy *endureth* forever.

Evening.

Minister. BLESS the LORD, O my soul: and all that is within me, *bless* his holy name.

Bless the LORD, O my soul, and forget not all his benefits:

People. Who forgiveth all thine iniquities; who healeth all thy diseases;

Who redeemeth thy life from destruction; who crowneth thee with lovingkindness and tender mercies;

M. Who satisfieth thy mouth with good *things; so that* thy youth is renewed like the eagle's.

P. The LORD executeth righteousness and judgment for all that are oppressed.

M. He made known his ways unto Moses, his acts unto the children of Israel.

P. The LORD *is* merciful and gracious, slow to anger, and plenteous in mercy.

He will not always chide : neither will he keep *his anger* forever.

M. He hath not dealt with us after our sins; nor rewarded us according to our iniquities.

P. For as the heaven is high above the earth, *so* great is his mercy toward them that fear him.

M. As far as the east is from the west, *so* far hath he removed our transgressions from us.

P. Like as a father pitieth *his* children, *so* the Lord pitieth them that fear him.

For he knoweth our frame; he remembereth that we *are* dust.

M. As for man, his days *are* as grass : as a flower of the field, so he flourisheth.

P. For the wind passeth over it, and it is gone; and the place thereof shall know it no more.

M. But the mercy of the Lord *is* from everlasting to everlasting upon them that fear him, and his righteousness unto children's children;

P. To such as keep his covenant, and to those that remember his commandments to do them.

EIGHTEENTH SABBATH.

Morning.

Minister. PRAISE ye the Lord. Sing unto the Lord a new song, *and* his praise in the congregation of saints.

People. Let Israel rejoice in him that made him: let the children of Zion be joyful in their King.

M. Let them praise his name in the dance: let them sing praises unto him with the timbrel and harp.

P. For the Lord taketh pleasure in his people: he will beautify the meek with salvation.

M. Let the saints be joyful in glory: let them sing aloud upon their beds.

P. Let the high *praises* of God *be* in their mouth, and a twoedged sword in their hand;

M. To execute vengeance upon the heathen, *and* punishments upon the people;

P. To bind their kings with chains, and their nobles with fetters of iron;

M. To execute upon them the judgment written: this honor have all his saints. Praise ye the LORD.

P. Praise ye the LORD. Praise God in his sanctuary: praise him in the firmament of his power.

M. Praise him for his mighty acts: praise him according to his excellent greatness.

P. Praise him with the sound of the trumpet: praise him with the psaltery and harp.

M. Praise him with the timbrel and

dance: praise him with stringed instruments and organs.

Praise him upon the loud cymbals: praise him upon the high sounding cymbals.

P. Let every thing that hath breath praise the LORD. Praise ye the LORD.

Evening.

Minister. O LORD, thou hast searched me, and known *me.*

Thou knowest my downsitting and mine uprising, thou understandest my thought afar off.

People. Thou compassest my path and my lying down, and art acquainted *with* all my ways.

M. For *there is* not a word in my tongue, *but* lo, O LORD, thou knowest it altogether.

Thou hast beset me behind and before, and laid thine hand upon me.

P. Such knowledge *is* too wonderful

for me; it is high, I cannot *attain* unto it.

M. Whither shall I go from thy Spirit? or whither shall I flee from thy presence?

If I ascend up into heaven, thou *art* there: if I make my bed in hell, behold, thou *art there.*

P. If I take the wings of the morning, *and* dwell in the uttermost parts of the sea;

M. Even there shall thy hand lead me, and thy right hand shall hold me.

P. If I say, Surely the darkness shall cover me; even the night shall be light about me.

M. Yea, the darkness hideth not from thee; but the night shineth as the day: the darkness and the light *are* both alike *to thee.*

P. Thine eyes did see my substance, yet being unperfect; and in thy book all *my members* were writ ten, *which* in continuance were fashioned, when *as yet there was* none of them.

M. How precious also are thy thoughts unto me, O God! how great is the sum of them!

P. If I should count them, they are more in number than the sand: when I awake, I am still with thee.

M. Search me, O God, and know my heart: try me, and know my thoughts:

P. And see if *there be any* wicked way in me, and lead me in the way everlasting.

NINETEENTH SABBATH.

Morning.

Minister. PRAISE ye the LORD. Praise the LORD, O my soul.

While I live will I praise the LORD:

I will sing praises unto my God while I have any being.

People. Put not your trust in princes, *nor* in the son of man, in whom *there is* no help.

M. His breath goeth forth, he returneth to his earth; in that very day his thoughts perish.

P. The LORD *is* righteous in all his ways, and holy in all his works.

M. The LORD *is* nigh unto all them that call upon him, to all that call upon him in truth.

P. He will fulfil the desire of them that fear him: he also will hear their cry, and will save them.

M. The LORD preserveth all them that love him: but all the wicked will he destroy.

P. My mouth shall speak the praise of the LORD: and let all flesh bless his holy name for ever and ever.

M. The LORD openeth *the eyes of* the blind: the LORD raiseth them that are bowed down: the Lord loveth the righteous:

P. The Lord 'preserveth the strangers; he relieveth the fatherless and widow: but the way of the wicked he turneth upside down.

M. Praise ye the Lord: for *it is* good to sing praises unto our God; for *it is* pleasant; *and* praise is comely.

P. The Lord doth build up Jerusalem: he gathereth together the outcasts of Israel.

He healeth the broken in heart, and bindeth up their wounds.

M. He telleth the number of the stars; he calleth them all by *their* names.

P. Great *is* our Lord, and of great power: his understanding *is* infinite.

Evening.

Minister. HEAR my prayer, O Lord, give ear to my supplications: in thy faithfulness answer me, *and* in thy righteousness.

And enter not into judgment with thy servant: for in thy sight shall no man living be justified.

People. For the enemy hath persecuted my soul; he hath smitten my life down to the ground; he hath made me to dwell in darkness, as those that have been long dead.

M. Therefore is my spirit overwhelmed within me; my heart within me is desolate.

I remember the days of old, I meditate on all thy works; I muse on the work of thy hands.

P. I stretch forth my hands unto thee: my soul *thirsteth* after thee, as a thirsty land.

M. Hear me speedily, O Lord: my spirit faileth: hide not thy face from me, lest I be like unto them that go down into the pit.

P. Cause me to hear thy lovingkindness in the morning; for in thee do I trust: cause me to know the way wherein I should walk; for I lift up my soul unto thee.

M. Deliver me, O LORD, from mine enemies: I flee unto thee to hide me.

Teach me to do thy will; for thou *art* my God: thy spirit *is* good; lead me into the land of uprightness.

P. Quicken me, O LORD, for thy name's sake: for thy righteousness' sake bring my soul out of trouble.

M. Out of the depths have I cried unto thee, O LORD.

Lord, hear my voice: let thine ears be attentive to the voice of my supplications.

P. If thou, LORD, shouldest mark iniquities, O Lord, who shall stand?

M. But *there is* forgiveness with thee, that thou mayest be feared.

I wait for the LORD, my soul doth wait, and in his word do I hope.

P. My soul *waiteth* for the Lord

more than they that watch for the morning: *I say, more than* they that watch for the morning.

M. Let Israel hope in the LORD: for with the LORD *there is* mercy, and with him *is* plenteous redemption.

P. And he shall redeem Israel from all his iniquities.

TWENTIETH SABBATH.

Morning.

Minister. O LORD our Lord, how excellent *is* thy name in all the earth!

People. Arise, O LORD; let not man prevail: let the heathen be judged in thy sight.

M. Put them in fear, O LORD: *that* the nations may know themselves *to be but* men.

P. Preserve me, O God: for in thee do I put my trust.

M. *O my soul*, thou hast said unto the Lord, Thou *art* my Lord: my goodness *extendeth* not to thee;

P. *But* to the saints that *are* in the earth, and *to* the excellent, in whom *is* all my delight.

M. Their sorrows shall be multiplied *that* hasten *after* another *god:* their drink offerings of blood will I not offer, nor take up their names into my lips.

P. The Lord *is* the portion of mine inheritance and of my cup: thou maintainest my lot.

M. The lines are fallen unto me in pleasant *places;* yea, I have a goodly heritage.

P. I will bless the Lord, who hath given me counsel: my reins also instruct me in the night seasons.

M. I have set the Lord always before me: because *he is* at my right hand, I shall not be moved.

P. Therefore my heart is glad, and

my glory rejoiceth : my flesh also shall rest in hope.

M. For thou wilt not leave my soul in hell; neither wilt thou suffer thine Holy One to see corruption.

P. Thou wilt show me the path of life : in thy presence *is* fulness of joy; at thy right hand *there are* pleasures for evermore.

Evening.

Minister. I WILL lift up mine eyes unto the hills, from whence cometh my help.

People. My help *cometh* from the LORD, which made heaven and earth.

M. He will not suffer thy foot to be moved : he that keepeth thee will not slumber.

P. Behold, he that keepeth Israel shall neither slumber nor sleep.

M. The LORD *is* thy keeper: the LORD *is* thy shade upon thy right hand.

P. The sun shall not smite thee by day, nor the moon by night.

M. The Lord shall preserve thee from all evil: he shall preserve thy soul.

P. The Lord shall preserve thy going out and thy coming in from this time forth, and even for evermore.

M. When the Lord turned again the captivity of Zion, we were like them that dream.

P. Then was our mouth filled with laughter, and our tongue with singing: then said they among the heathen, The Lord hath done great things for them.

M. The Lord hath done great things for us; *whereof* we are glad.

P. Turn again our captivity, O Lord, as the streams in the south.

M. They that sow in tears shall reap in joy.

P. He that goeth forth and weepeth, bearing precious seed, shall doubtless come again with rejoicing, bringing his sheaves *with him.*

TWENTY-FIRST SABBATH.

Morning.

Minister. HAVE mercy upon me, O God, according to thy lovingkindness: according unto the multitude of thy tender mercies blot out my transgressions.

People. Wash me thoroughly from mine iniquity, and cleanse me from my sin.

For I acknowledge my transgressions: and my sin *is* ever before me.

M. Against thee, thee only, have I sinned, and done *this* evil in thy sight: that thou mightest be justified when thou speakest, *and* be clear when thou judgest.

P. Purge me with hyssop, and I shall be clean: wash me, and I shall be whiter than snow.

Make me to hear joy and gladness; *that* the bones *which* thou hast broken may rejoice.

M. Hide thy face from my sins, and blot out all mine iniquities.

P. Create in me a clean heart, O God; and renew a right spirit within me.

M. Cast me not away from thy presence; and take not thy Holy Spirit from me.

P. Restore unto me the joy of thy salvation; and uphold me *with thy* free Spirit.

Then will I teach transgressors thy ways; and sinners shall be converted unto thee.

M. Deliver me from bloodguiltiness, O God, thou God of my salvation: *and* my tongue shall sing aloud of thy righteousness.

P. O Lord, open thou my lips; and my mouth shall show forth thy praise.

M. For thou desirest not sacrifice; else would I give *it;* thou delightest not in burnt offering.

P. The sacrifices of God *are* a broken spirit: a broken and a contrite heart, O God, thou wilt not despise.

M. Do good in thy good pleasure unto Zion: build thou the walls of Jerusalem.

P. Then shalt thou be pleased with the sacrifices of righteousness, with burnt offering and whole burnt offering: then shall they offer bullocks upon thine altar.

Evening.

Minister. THE LORD said unto my Lord, Sit thou at my right hand, until I make thine enemies thy footstool.

People. The LORD shall send the rod

of thy strength out of Zion: rule thou in the midst of thine enemies.

M. Thy people *shall be* willing in the day of thy power, in the beauties of holiness from the womb of the morning: thou hast the dew of thy youth.

P. The LORD hath sworn, and will not repent, Thou *art* a priest forever after the order of Melchizedek.

M. The Lord at thy right hand shall strike through kings in the day of his wrath.

P. He shall judge among the heathen, he shall fill *the places* with the dead bodies; he shall wound the heads over many countries.

M. He shall drink of the brook in the way: therefore shall he lift up the head.

P. They shall speak of the glory of thy kingdom, and talk of thy power;

M. To make known to the sons of men his mighty acts, and the glorious majesty of his kingdom.

P. Thy kingdom *is* an everlasting

kingdom, and thy dominion *endureth* throughout all generations.

M. The LORD hath sworn *in* truth unto David; he will not turn from it; Of the fruit of thy body will I set upon thy throne.

P. If thy children will keep my covenant and my testimony that I shall teach them, their children shall also sit upon thy throne for evermore.

M. For the LORD hath chosen Zion; he hath desired *it* for his habitation.

P. This *is* my rest forever: here will I dwell; for I have desired it.

TWENTY-SECOND SABBATH.

Morning.

Minister. THE mighty God, *even* the LORD, hath spoken, and called the earth from the rising of the sun unto the going down thereof.

People. Out of Zion, the perfection of beauty, God hath shined.

M. Our God shall come, and shall not keep silence: a fire shall devour before him, and it shall be very tempestuous round about him.

P. He shall call to the heavens from above, and to the earth, that he may judge his people.

M. Gather my saints together unto me; those that have made a covenant with me by sacrifice.

P. And the heavens shall declare his righteousness: for God *is* judge himself.

M. Offer unto God thanksgiving; and pay thy vows unto the Most High:

P. And call upon me in the day of trouble: I will deliver thee, and thou shalt glorify me.

M. Whoso offereth praise glorifieth me: and to him that ordereth *his* conversation *aright* will I show the salvation of God.

P. Make a joyful noise unto the LORD, all ye lands.

M. Serve the LORD with gladness: come before his presence with singing.

P. Know ye that the LORD he *is* God: *it is* he *that* hath made us, and not we ourselves; *we are* his people, and the sheep of his pasture.

M. Enter into his gates with thanksgiving, *and* into his courts with praise: be thankful unto him, *and* bless his name.

P. For the LORD *is* good; his mercy *is* everlasting; and his truth *endureth* to all generations.

Evening.

Minister. UNTO thee will I cry, O LORD my rock; be not silent to me: lest, *if* thou be silent to me, I become like them that go down into the pit.

People. Hear the voice of my supplications, when I cry unto thee, when I lift up my hands toward thy holy oracle.

M. Draw me not away with the wicked, and with the workers of iniquity, which speak peace to their neighbors, but mischief *is* in their hearts.

P. Give them according to their deeds, and according to the wickedness of their endeavors: give them after the work of their hands; render to them their desert.

M. In my prosperity I said, I shall never be moved.

P. LORD, by thy favor thou hast made my mountain to stand strong: thou didst hide thy face, *and* I was troubled.

M. I cried to thee, O LORD; and unto the LORD I made supplication.

P. What profit *is there* in my blood, when I go down to the pit? Shall the dust praise thee? shall it declare thy truth?

M. Hear, O Lord, and have mercy upon me: Lord, be thou my helper.

P. Thou hast turned for me my mourning into dancing: thou hast put off my sackcloth, and girded me with gladness.

M. Blessed *be* the Lord, because he hath heard the voice of my supplications.

P. The Lord *is* my strength, and my shield; my heart trusted in him, and I am helped: therefore my heart greatly rejoiceth; and with my song will I praise him.

M. The Lord *is* their strength, and he *is* the saving strength of his anointed.

P. Save thy people, and bless thine inheritance: feed them also, and lift them up forever.

TWENTY-THIRD SABBATH.

Morning.

Minister. GREAT *is* the LORD, and greatly to be praised in the city of our God, *in* the mountain of his holiness.

People. Beautiful for situation, the joy of the whole earth, *is* mount Zion, *on* the sides of the north, the city of the great King.

M. God is known in her palaces for a refuge.

P. For, lo, the kings were assembled, they passed by together.

M. They saw *it, and* so they marvelled; they were troubled, *and* hasted away.

P. Fear took hold upon them there, *and* pain, as of a woman in travail.

M. Thou breakest the ships of Tarshish with an east wind.

P. As we have heard, so have we

seen in the city of the Lord of hosts, in the city of our God: God will establish it forever.

M. We have thought of thy lovingkindness, O God, in the midst of thy temple.

P. According to thy name, O God, so *is* thy praise unto the ends of the earth: thy right hand is full of righteousness.

M. Let mount Zion rejoice, let the daughters of Judah be glad, because of thy judgments.

P. Walk about Zion, and go round about her: tell the towers thereof.

M. Mark ye well her bulwarks, consider her palaces; that ye may tell *it* to the generation following.

P. For this God *is* our God for ever and ever: he will be our guide *even* unto death.

Evening.

Minister. YE that fear the LORD, praise him; all ye the seed of Jacob, glorify him; and fear him, all ye the seed of Israel.

People. For he hath not despised nor abhorred the affliction of the afflicted; neither hath he hid his face from him; but when he cried unto him, he heard.

M. My praise *shall be* of thee in the great congregation: I will pay my vows before them that fear him.

P. The meek shall eat and be satisfied: they shall praise the LORD that seek him: your heart shall live forever.

M. All the ends of the world shall remember and turn unto the LORD: and all the kindreds of the nations shall worship before thee.

P. For the kingdom *is* the LORD's: and he *is* the governor among the nations.

M. All *they that be* fat upon earth shall eat and worship: all they that go down to the dust shall bow before him: and none can keep alive his own soul.

P. A seed shall serve him; it shall be accounted to the Lord for a generation.

M. They shall come, and shall declare his righteousness unto a people that shall be born, that he hath done *this.*

P. Know that the Lord hath set apart him that is godly for himself: the Lord will hear when I call unto him.

M. Stand in awe, and sin not: commune with your own heart upon your bed, and be still.

Offer the sacrifices of righteousness, and put your trust in the Lord.

P. There be many that say, Who will show us *any* good? Lord, lift thou up the light of thy countenance upon us.

M. Thou hast put gladness in my heart, more than in the time *that* their corn and their wine increased.

P. I will both lay me down in peace, and sleep: for thou, LORD, only makest me dwell in safety.

TWENTY-FOURTH SABBATH.

Morning.

Minister. GIRD thy sword upon thy thigh, O *most* Mighty, with thy glory and thy majesty.

People. And in thy majesty ride prosperously, because of truth and meekness *and* righteousness; and thy right hand shall teach thee terrible things.

M. Thine arrows *are* sharp in the heart of the King's enemies; *whereby* the people fall under thee.

P. Thy throne, O God, *is* for ever and ever: the sceptre of thy kingdom *is* a right sceptre.

M. Thou lovest righteousness, and hatest wickedness: therefore God, thy God, hath anointed thee with the oil of gladness above thy fellows.

P. All thy garments *smell* of myrrh, and aloes, *and* cassia, out of the ivory palaces, whereby they have made thee glad.

M. Kings' daughters *were* among thy honorable women: upon thy right hand did stand the queen in gold of Ophir.

P. Hearken, O daughter, and consider, and incline thine ear; forget also thine own people, and thy father's house;

M. So shall the King greatly desire thy beauty: for he *is* thy Lord; and worship thou him.

P. And the daughter of Tyre *shall be there* with a gift; *even* the rich among the people shall entreat thy favor.

M. The King's daughter *is* all glorious within: her clothing *is* of wrought gold.

She shall be brought unto the King in raiment of needlework: the virgins her companions that follow her shall be brought unto thee.

P. With gladness and rejoicing shall they be brought: they shall enter into the King's palace.

M. Instead of thy fathers shall be thy children, whom thou mayest make princes in all the earth.

P. I will make thy name to be remembered in all generations: therefore shall the people praise thee for ever and ever.

Evening.

Minister. MINE eyes *are* ever toward the LORD; for he shall pluck my feet out of the net.

Turn thee unto me, and have mercy upon me; for I *am* desolate and afflicted.

People. The troubles of my heart are enlarged: *oh* bring thou me out of my distresses.

M. Look upon mine affliction and my pain; and forgive all my sins.

P. Consider mine enemies; for they are many; and they hate me with cruel hatred.

M. Oh keep my soul, and deliver me: let me not be ashamed; for I put my trust in thee.

P. Let integrity and uprightness preserve me; for I wait on thee.

Redeem Israel, O God, out of all his troubles.

M. Judge me, O Lord; for I have walked in mine integrity: I have trusted also in the Lord; *therefore* I shall not slide.

P. Examine me, O Lord, and prove me; try my reins and my heart.

For thy lovingkindness *is* before

mine eyes: and I have walked in thy truth.

M. I have not sat with vain persons, neither will I go in with dissemblers.

I have hated the congregation of evil doers; and will not sit with the wicked.

P. I will wash mine hands in innocency: so will I compass thine altar, O LORD:

That I may publish with the voice of thanksgiving, and tell of all thy wondrous works.

M. LORD, I have loved the habitation of thy house, and the place where thine honor dwelleth.

P. Gather not my soul with sinners, nor my life with bloody men:

In whose hands *is* mischief, and their right hand is full of bribes.

M. But as for me, I will walk in mine integrity: redeem me, and be merciful unto me.

P. My foot standeth in an even place: in the congregations will I bless the Lord.

TWENTY-FIFTH SABBATH.

Morning.

Minister. REJOICE in the Lord, O ye righteous: *for* praise is comely for the upright.

People. Praise the Lord with harp: sing unto him with the psaltery *and* an instrument of ten strings.

M. Sing unto him a new song; play skilfully with a loud noise.

For the word of the Lord *is* right; and all his works *are done* in truth.

P. He loveth righteousness and judgment: the earth is full of the goodness of the Lord.

M. By the word of the Lord were the heavens made; and all the host of them by the breath of his mouth.

P. He gathereth the waters of the sea together as a heap: he layeth up the depth in storehouses.

M. Let all the earth fear the LORD: let all the inhabitants of the world stand in awe of him.

For he spake, and it was *done;* he commanded, and it stood fast.

P. The LORD bringeth the counsel of the heathen to nought: he maketh the devices of the people of none effect.

The counsel of the LORD standeth forever, the thoughts of his heart to all generations.

M. Blessed *is* the nation whose God *is* the LORD; *and* the people *whom* he hath chosen for his own inheritance.

P. Behold, the eye of the LORD *is* upon them that fear him, upon them that hope in his mercy;

M. To deliver their soul from death, and to keep them alive in famine.

P. Our soul waiteth for the LORD: he *is* our help and our shield.

M. For our heart shall rejoice in him, because we have trusted in his holy name.

P. Let thy mercy, O LORD, be upon us, according as we hope in thee.

Evening.

Minister. THOU *art* holy, *O thou* that inhabitest the praises of Israel.

People. Our fathers trusted in thee: they trusted, and thou didst deliver them.

M. They cried unto thee, and were delivered: they trusted in thee, and were not confounded.

P. The LORD hear thee in the day of trouble; the name of the God of Jacob defend thee;

M. Send thee help from the sanctuary, and strengthen thee out of Zion;

P. Remember all thy offerings, and accept thy burnt-sacrifice;

M. Grant thee according to thine own heart, and fulfil all thy counsel.

P. We will rejoice in thy salvation, and in the name of our God we will set up *our* banners: the LORD fulfil all thy petitions.

M. Now know I that the LORD saveth his anointed; he will hear him from his holy heaven with the saving strength of his right hand.

P. Some *trust* in chariots, and some in horses: but we will remember the name of the LORD our God.

M. They are brought down and fallen: but we are risen, and stand upright.

P. Save, LORD: let the king hear us when we call.

Deliver my soul from the sword, my darling from the power of the dog.

M. Save me from the lion's mouth:

for thou hast heard me from the horns of the unicorns.

P. I will declare thy name unto my brethren: in the midst of the congregation will I praise thee.

TWENTY-SIXTH SABBATH.

Morning.

Minister. THE LORD *is* my light and my salvation; whom shall I fear? the LORD *is* the strength of my life; of whom shall I be afraid?

People. When the wicked, *even* mine enemies and my foes, came upon me to eat up my flesh, they stumbled and fell.

M. Though a host should encamp against me, my heart shall not fear: though war should rise against me, in this *will* I *be* confident.

P. One *thing* have I desired of the LORD, that will I seek after; that I may dwell in the house of the LORD all the days of my life, to behold the beauty of the LORD, and to inquire in his temple.

M. For in the time of trouble he shall hide me in his pavilion: in the secret of his tabernacle shall he hide me; he shall set me up upon a rock.

P. And now shall mine head be lifted up above mine enemies round about me: therefore will I offer in his tabernacle sacrifices of joy; I will sing, yea, I will sing praises unto the LORD.

M. Hear, O LORD, *when* I cry with my voice: have mercy also upon me, and answer me.

P. When thou saidst, Seek ye my face; my heart said unto thee, Thy face, LORD, will I seek.

M. Hide not thy face *far* from me; put not thy servant away in anger: thou hast been my help; leave me not, neither forsake me, O God of my salvation.

P. When my father and my mother forsake me, then the LORD will take me up.

M. Teach me thy way, O LORD, and lead me in a plain path, because of mine enemies.

P. Deliver me not over unto the will of mine enemies: for false witnesses are risen up against me, and such as breathe out cruelty.

M. I had fainted, unless I had believed to see the goodness of the LORD in the land of the living.

P. Wait on the LORD: be of good courage, and he shall strengthen thine heart: wait, I say, on the LORD.

Evening.

Minister. O LORD my God, in thee do I put my trust: save me from all them that persecute me, and deliver me:

People. Lest he tear my soul like a lion, rending *it* in pieces, while *there is* none to deliver.

M. O LORD my God, if I have done this; if there be iniquity in my hands;

P. If I have rewarded evil unto him that was at peace with me; (yea, I have delivered him that without cause is mine enemy:)

M. Let the enemy persecute my soul and take *it;* yea, let him tread down my life upon the earth, and lay mine honor in the dust.

P. Arise, O LORD, in thine anger, lift up thyself because of the rage of mine enemies: and awake for me *to* the judgment *that* thou hast commanded.

M. So shall the congregation of the people compass thee about: for their sakes therefore return thou on high.

P. The LORD shall judge the people: judge me, O LORD, according to my righteousness, and according to mine integrity *that is* in me.

M. O let the wickedness of the wicked come to an end; but establish the just: for the righteous God trieth the hearts and reins.

P. My defence *is* of God, which saveth the upright in heart.

M. God judgeth the righteous, and God is angry *with the wicked* every day.

P. If he turn not, he will whet his sword; he hath bent his bow, and made it ready.

M. He hath also prepared for him the instruments of death; he ordaineth his arrows against the persecutors.

P. His mischief shall return upon his own head, and his violent dealing shall come down upon his own pate.

M. I will praise the LORD according to his righteousness: and will sing praise to the name of the LORD most high.

TWENTY-SEVENTH SABBATH.

Morning.

Minister. THE LORD reigneth; let the people tremble: he sitteth *between* the cherubims; let the earth be moved.

People. The LORD *is* great in Zion; and he *is* high above all people.

M. Let them praise thy great and terrible name; *for* it *is* holy.

P. The king's strength also loveth judgment; thou dost establish equity, thou executest judgment and righteousness in Jacob.

M. Exalt ye the LORD our God, and worship at his footstool; *for* he *is* holy.

P. Moses and Aaron among his priests, and Samuel among them that call upon his name; they called upon the LORD, and he answered them.

M. He spake unto them in the

cloudy pillar: they kept his testimonies, and the ordinance *that* he gave them.

P. Thou answeredst them, O Lord our God: thou wast a God that forgavest them, though thou tookest vengeance of their inventions.

M. Exalt the Lord our God, and worship at his holy hill; for the Lord our God *is* holy.

Blessed be the name of the Lord from this time forth and for evermore.

P. From the rising of the sun unto the going down of the same the Lord's name *is* to be praised.

M. The Lord *is* high above all nations, *and* his glory above the heavens.

P. Who *is* like unto the Lord our God, who dwelleth on high,

Who humbleth *himself* to behold *the things that are* in heaven, and in the earth!

M. He raiseth up the poor out of

the dust, *and* lifteth the needy out of the dunghill;

That he may set *him* with princes, *even* with the princes of his people.

P. He maketh the barren woman to keep house, *and to be* a joyful mother of children. Praise ye the LORD.

Evening.

Minister. O LORD God, to whom vengeance belongeth; O God, to whom vengeance belongeth, show thyself.

People. Lift up thyself, thou Judge of the earth: render a reward to the proud.

M. LORD, how long shall the wicked, how long shall the wicked triumph?

P. How long shall they utter *and* speak hard things? *and* all the workers of iniquity boast themselves?

M. They break in pieces thy people, O LORD, and afflict thine heritage.

They slay the widow and the stranger, and murder the fatherless.

P. Yet they say, The Lord shall not see, neither shall the God of Jacob regard *it.*

M. Understand, ye brutish among the people: and *ye* fools, when will ye be wise?

P. He that planted the ear, shall he not hear? he that formed the eye, shall he not see?

M. He that chastiseth the heathen, shall not he correct? he that teacheth man knowledge, *shall not he know?*

P. The Lord knoweth the thoughts of man, that they *are* vanity.

M. Blessed *is* the man whom thou chastenest, O Lord, and teachest him out of thy law;

P. That thou mayest give him rest from the days of adversity, until the pit be digged for the wicked.

M. For the Lord will not cast off his people, neither will he forsake his inheritance.

P. But judgment shall return unto righteousness: and all the upright in heart shall follow it.

TWENTY-EIGHTH SABBATH.

Morning.

Minister. THE LORD reigneth, he is clothed with majesty; the LORD is clothed with strength, *wherewith* he hath girded himself: the world also is stablished, that it cannot be moved.

People. Thy throne *is* established of old: thou *art* from everlasting.

M. Why do the heathen rage, and the people imagine a vain thing?

P. The kings of the earth set themselves, and the rulers take counsel together, against the LORD, and against his Anointed, *saying,*

M. Let us break their bands asunder, and cast away their cords from us.

P. He that sitteth in the heavens shall laugh: the Lord shall have them in derision.

M. Then shall he speak unto them in his wrath, and vex them in his sore displeasure.

P. Yet have I set my King upon my holy hill of Zion.

M. I will declare the decree: the LORD hath said unto me, Thou *art* my Son;. this day have I begotten thee.

P. Ask of me, and I shall give *thee* the heathen *for* thine inheritance, and the uttermost parts of the earth *for* thy possession.

M. Thou shalt break them with a rod of iron; thou shalt dash them in pieces like a potter's vessel.

P. Be wise now therefore, O ye kings: be instructed, ye judges of the earth.

M. Serve the Lord with fear, and rejoice with trembling.

P. Kiss the Son, lest he be angry, and ye perish *from* the way, when his wrath is kindled but a little. Blessed *are* all they that put their trust in him.

Evening.

Minister. PLEAD *my cause,* O Lord, with them that strive with me: fight against them that fight against me.

People. Take hold of shield and buckler, and stand up for mine help.

M. Draw out also the spear, and stop *the way* against them that persecute me: say unto my soul, I *am* thy salvation.

P. Let them be confounded and put to shame that seek after my soul: let them be turned back and brought to confusion that devise my hurt.

M. Let them be as chaff before the

wind: and let the angel of the Lord chase *them*.

P. Let their way be dark and slippery: and let the angel of the Lord persecute them.

M. For without cause have they hid for me their net *in* a pit, *which* without cause they have digged for my soul.

P. Let destruction come upon him at unawares; and let his net that he hath hid catch himself: into that very destruction let him fall.

M. Save me, O God, by thy name, and judge me by thy strength.

Hear my prayer, O God: give ear to the words of my mouth.

P. For strangers are risen up against me, and oppressors seek after my soul: they have not set God before them.

M. Behold, God *is* mine helper: the Lord *is* with them that uphold my soul.

P. He shall reward evil unto mine enemies; cut them off in thy truth.

M. I will freely sacrifice unto thee : I will praise thy name, O LORD; for *it is* good.

P. For he hath delivered me out of all trouble : and mine eye hath seen *his desire* upon mine enemies.

TWENTY-NINTH SABBATH.

Morning.

Minister. NOT unto us, O LORD, not unto us, but unto thy name give glory, for thy mercy, *and* for thy truth's sake.

People. Wherefore should the heathen say, Where *is* now their God?

M. But our God *is* in the heavens: he hath done whatsoever he hath pleased.

P. Their idols *are* silver and gold, the work of men's hands.

They have mouths, but they speak

not: eyes have they, but they see not:

M. They have ears, but they hear not: noses have they, but they smell not:

They have hands, but they handle not: feet have they, but they walk not: neither speak they through their throat.

P. They that make them are like unto them; *so is* every one that trusteth in them.

M. O Israel, trust thou in the LORD: he *is* their help and their shield.

P. O house of Aaron, trust in the LORD: he *is* their help and their shield.

M. Ye that fear the LORD, trust in the LORD: he *is* their help and their shield.

P. The LORD hath been mindful of us: he will bless *us;* he will bless the house of Israel: he will bless the house of Aaron.

M. He will bless them that fear the Lord, *both* small and great.

P. The Lord shall increase you more and more, you and your children.

Ye *are* blessed of the Lord which made heaven and earth.

M. The heaven, *even* the heavens, *are* the Lord's: but the earth hath he given to the children of men.

P. The dead praise not the Lord, neither any that go down into silence.

But we will bless the Lord from this time forth and for evermore. Praise the Lord.

Evening.

Minister. ARISE, O Lord; O God, lift up thine hand: forget not the humble.

People. Wherefore doth the wicked contemn God? he hath said in his heart, Thou wilt not require *it.*

M. Thou hast seen *it;* for thou beholdest mischief and spite, to requite *it* with thy hand: the poor committeth himself unto thee; thou art the helper of the fatherless.

P. Break thou the arm of the wicked and the evil *man:* seek out his wickedness *till* thou find none.

M. The Lord *is* King for ever and ever: the heathen are perished out of his land.

P. Lord, thou hast heard the desire of the humble: thou wilt prepare their heart, thou wilt cause thine ear to hear:

M. To judge the fatherless and the oppressed, that the man of the earth may no more oppress.

P. Hear my cry, O God; attend unto my prayer.

M. From the end of the earth will I cry unto thee, when my heart is overwhelmed: lead me to the rock *that* is higher than I.

P. For thou hast been a shelter for me, *and* a strong tower from the enemy.

M. I will abide in thy tabernacle for ever: I will trust in the covert of thy wings.

P. For thou, O God, hast heard my vows: thou hast given *me* the heritage of those that fear thy name.

M. Thou wilt prolong the king's life: *and* his years as many generations.

P. He shall abide before God forever: oh prepare mercy and truth, *which* may preserve him.

M. So will I sing praise unto thy name forever, that I may daily perform my vows.

THIRTIETH SABBATH.

Morning.

Minister. THE LORD reigneth; let the earth rejoice; let the multitude of isles be glad *thereof.*

People. Clouds and darkness *are* round about him: righteousness and judgment *are* the habitation of his throne.

M. A fire goeth before him, and burneth up his enemies round about.

His lightnings enlightened the world: the earth saw, and trembled.

P. The hills melted like wax at the presence of the Lord, at the presence of the Lord of the whole earth.

M. The heavens declare his righteousness, and all the people see his glory.

P. Confounded be all they that serve graven images, that boast themselves of idols: worship him, all *ye* gods.

M. Zion heard, and was glad; and the daughters of Judah rejoiced because of thy judgments, O Lord.

P. For thou, Lord, *art* high above all the earth: thou art exalted far above all gods.

M. Ye that love the Lord, hate evil: he preserveth the souls of his saints; he delivereth them out of the hand of the wicked.

P. Light is sown for the righteous, and gladness for the upright in heart.

M. Rejoice in the Lord, ye righteous; and give thanks at the remembrance of his holiness.

P. O sing unto the Lord a new song; for he hath done marvellous things: his right hand, and his holy arm, hath gotten him the victory.

M. The Lord hath made known his salvation: his righteousness hath he openly showed in the sight of the heathen.

P. He hath remembered his mercy and his truth toward the house of Israel: all the ends of the earth have seen the salvation of our God.

Evening.

Minister. BEHOLD, I was shapen in iniquity; and in sin did my mother conceive me.

People. Behold, thou desirest truth in the inward parts: and in the hidden *part* thou shalt make me to know wisdom.

M. Purge me with hyssop, and I shall be clean: wash me, and I shall be whiter than snow.

P. Truly my soul waiteth upon God: from him *cometh* my salvation.

M. He only *is* my rock and my salvation; *he is* my defence; I shall not be greatly moved.

P. How long will ye imagine mischief against a man? ye shall be slain all of you: as a bowing wall *shall ye be, and as* a tottering fence.

M. They only consult to cast *him* down from his excellency: they delight in lies: they bless with their mouth, but they curse inwardly.

P. My soul, wait thou only upon God; for my expectation *is* from him.

M. He only *is* my rock and my salvation: *he is* my defence; I shall not be moved.

P. In God *is* my salvation and my glory: the rock of my strength, *and* my refuge, *is* in God.

M. Trust in him at all times; ye people, pour out your heart before him: God *is* a refuge for us.

P. Surely men of low degree *are* vanity, *and* men of high degree *are* a lie: to be laid in the balance, they *are* altogether *lighter* than vanity.

M. Trust not in oppression, and become not vain in robbery: if riches increase, set not your heart *upon them.*

P. God hath spoken once; twice have I heard this; that power *belongeth* unto God.

M. Also unto thee, O Lord, *belongeth* mercy: for thou renderest to every man according to his work.

THIRTY-FIRST SABBATH.

Morning.

Minister. OH come, let us sing unto the Lord: let us make a joyful noise to the Rock of our salvation.

People. Let us come before his presence with thanksgiving, and make a joyful noise unto him with psalms.

M. For the Lord *is* a great God, and a great King above all gods.

P. Those that be planted in the house of the Lord shall flourish in the courts of our God.

M. They shall still bring forth fruit in old age; they shall be fat and flourishing;

P. To show that the Lord *is* upright: *he is* my rock, and *there is* no unrighteousness in him.

M. In his hand *are* the deep places

of the earth: the strength of the hills *is* his also.

P. The sea *is* his, and he made it: and his hands formed the dry *land.*

M. Oh come, let us worship and bow down: let us kneel before the LORD our maker.

P. For he *is* our God; and we *are* the people of his pasture, and the sheep of his hand. To day if ye will hear his voice,

M. Harden not your heart, as in the provocation, *and* as *in* the day of temptation in the wilderness:

P. When your fathers tempted me, proved me, and saw my work.

M. Forty years long was I grieved with *this* generation, and said, It *is* a people that do err in their heart, and they have not known my ways:

P. Unto whom I sware in my wrath that they should not enter into my rest.

Evening.

Minister. UNTO thee lift I up mine eyes, O thou that dwellest in the heavens.

People. Behold, as the eyes of servants *look* unto the hand of their masters, *and* as the eyes of a maiden unto the hand of her mistress; so our eyes *wait* upon the LORD our God, until that he have mercy upon us.

M. Have mercy upon us, O LORD, have mercy upon us: for we are exceedingly filled with contempt.

P. Our soul is exceedingly filled with the scorning of those that are at ease, *and* with the contempt of the proud.

M. If *it had* not *been* the LORD who was on our side, now may Israel say;

If *it had* not *been* the LORD who was on our side, when men rose up against us:

P. Then they had swallowed us up quick, when their wrath was kindled against us:

M. Then the waters had overwhelmed us, the stream had gone over our soul:

P. Then the proud waters had gone over our soul.

M. Blessed *be* the LORD, who hath not given us *as* a prey to their teeth.

P. Our soul is escaped as a bird out of the snare of the fowlers: the snare is broken, and we are escaped.

M. Our help *is* in the name of the LORD, who made heaven and earth.

P. For the rod of the wicked shall not rest upon the lot of the righteous; lest the righteous put forth their hands unto iniquity.

M. Do good, O LORD, unto *those that be* good, and to *them that are* upright in their hearts.

P. As for such as turn aside unto their crooked ways, the LORD shall lead them forth with the workers of iniquity: *but* peace *shall be* upon Israel.

THIRTY-SECOND SABBATH.

Morning.

Minister. GOD standeth in the congregation of the mighty; he judgeth among the gods.

People. How long will ye judge unjustly, and accept the persons of the wicked?

M. Defend the poor and fatherless: do justice to the afflicted and needy.

P. Deliver the poor and needy: rid *them* out of the hand of the wicked.

M. They know not, neither will they understand; they walk on in darkness: all the foundations of the earth are out of course.

P. I have said, Ye *are* gods; and all of you are children of the Most High.

M. But ye shall die like men, and fall like one of the princes.

P. Arise, O God, judge the earth: for thou shalt inherit all nations.

M. Many *there be* which say of my soul, *There is* no help for him in God.

P. But thou, O Lord, *art* a shield for me; my glory, and the lifter up of mine head.

M. I cried unto the Lord with my voice, and he heard me out of his holy hill.

I laid me down and slept; I awaked; for the Lord sustained me.

P. I will not be afraid of ten thousands of people, that have set *themselves* against me round about.

M. Arise, O Lord; save me, O my God: for thou hast smitten all mine enemies *upon* the cheek bone; thou hast broken the teeth of the ungodly.

P. Salvation *belongeth* unto the Lord: thy blessing *is* upon thy people.

Evening.

Minister. GIVE ear to my words, O Lord; consider my meditation.

People. Hearken unto the voice of my cry, my King, and my God: for unto thee will I pray.

M. My voice shalt thou hear in the morning, O Lord; in the morning will I direct *my prayer* unto thee, and will look up.

P. For thou *art* not a God that hath pleasure in wickedness: neither shall evil dwell with thee.

M. The foolish shall not stand in thy sight: thou hatest all workers of iniquity.

P. Thou shalt destroy them that speak leasing: the Lord will abhor the bloody and deceitful man.

M. But as for me, I will come *into* thy house in the multitude of thy mercy: *and* in thy fear will I worship toward thy holy temple.

P. Lead me, O Lord, in thy righteousness because of mine enemies; make thy way straight before my face.

M. For *there is* no faithfulness in

their mouth; their inward part *is* very wickedness; their throat *is* an open sepulchre; they flatter with their tongue.

P. Destroy thou them, O God; let them fall by their own counsels; cast them out in the multitude of their transgressions; for they have rebelled against thee.

M. But let all those that put their trust in thee rejoice: let them ever shout for joy, because thou defendest them: let them also that love thy name be joyful in thee.

P. For thou, Lord, wilt bless the righteous; with favor wilt thou compass him as *with* a shield.

M. Lord, my heart is not haughty, nor mine eyes lofty: neither do I exercise myself in great matters, or in things too high for me.

P. Let Israel hope in the Lord from henceforth and forever.

THIRTY-THIRD SABBATH.

Morning.

Minister. AS the hart panteth after the water brooks, so panteth my soul after thee, O God.

People. My soul thirsteth for God, for the living God: when shall I come and appear before God?

M. My tears have been my meat day and night, while they continually say unto me, Where *is* thy God?

P. When I remember these *things*, I pour out my soul in me: for I had gone with the multitude, I went with them to the house of God, with the voice of joy and praise, with a multitude that kept holyday.

M. Why art thou cast down, O my soul? and *why* art thou disquieted in me? hope thou in God: for I shall yet praise him *for* the help of his countenance.

P. Deep calleth unto deep at the noise of thy waterspouts: all thy waves and thy billows are gone over me.

M. Yet the LORD will command his lovingkindness in the daytime, and in the night his song *shall be* with me, *and* my prayer unto the God of my life.

P. I will say unto God my rock, Why hast thou forgotten me? why go I mourning because of the oppression of the enemy?

M. As with a sword in my bones, mine enemies reproach me; while they say daily unto me, Where *is* thy God?

P. Why art thou cast down, O my soul? and why art thou disquieted within me? hope thou in God: for I shall yet praise him, *who is* the health of my countenance, and my God.

M. Judge me, O God, and plead my cause against an ungodly nation: O deliver me from the deceitful and unjust man.

P. O send out thy light and thy truth: let them lead me; let them bring me unto thy holy hill, and to thy tabernacles.

M. Then will I go unto the altar of God, unto God my exceeding joy: yea, upon the harp will I praise thee, O God my God.

P. Why art thou cast down, O my soul? and why art thou disquieted within me? hope in God: for I shall yet praise him, *who is* the health of my countenance, and my God.

Evening.

Minister. THE heavens declare the glory of God; and the firmament showeth his handywork.

People. Day unto day uttereth speech, and night unto night showeth knowledge.

M. There is no speech nor language, *where* their voice is not heard.

P. Their line is gone out through all the earth, and their words to the end of the world. In them hath he set a tabernacle for the sun,

M. Which *is* as a bridegroom coming out of his chamber, *and* rejoiceth as a strong man to run a race.

P. His going forth *is* from the end of the heaven, and his circuit unto the ends of it: and there is nothing hid from the heat thereof.

M. The law of the Lord *is* perfect, converting the soul: the testimony of the Lord *is* sure, making wise the simple.

P. The statutes of the Lord *are* right, rejoicing the heart: the commandment of the Lord *is* pure, enlightening the eyes.

M. The fear of the Lord *is* clean, enduring forever: the judgments of the Lord *are* true *and* righteous altogether.

P. More to be desired *are they* than

gold, yea, than much fine gold: sweeter also than honey and the honeycomb.

M. Moreover by them is thy servant warned: *and* in keeping of them *there is* great reward.

P. Who can understand *his* errors? cleanse thou me from secret *faults.*

M. Keep back thy servant also from presumptuous *sins;* let them not have dominion over me: then shall I be upright, and I shall be innocent from the great transgression.

P. Let the words of my mouth, and the meditation of my heart, be acceptable in thy sight, O Lord, my strength, and my redeemer.

THIRTY-FOURTH SABBATH.

Morning.

Minister. O LORD our Lord, how excellent *is* thy name in all the earth! who hast set thy glory above the heavens.

People. Out of the mouth of babes and sucklings hast thou ordained strength because of thine enemies, that thou mightest still the enemy and the avenger.

M. When I consider thy heavens, the work of thy fingers, the moon and the stars, which thou hast ordained;

P. What is man, that thou art mindful of him? and the son of man, that thou visitest him?

M. For thou hast made him a little lower than the angels, and hast crowned him with glory and honor.

P. Thou madest him to have dominion over the works of thy hands; thou hast put all *things* under his feet:

M. All sheep and oxen, yea, and the beasts of the field;

P. The fowl of the air, and the fish of the sea, *and whatsoever* passeth through the paths of the seas.

M. O LORD our Lord, how excellent *is* thy name in all the earth!

P. Lord, who shall abide in thy tabernacle? who shall dwell in thy holy hill?

M. He that walketh uprightly, and worketh righteousness, and speaketh the truth in his heart.

P. He that backbiteth not with his tongue, nor doeth evil to his neighbor, nor taketh up a reproach against his neighbor.

M. In whose eyes a vile person is contemned; but he honoreth them that fear the Lord. *He that* sweareth to *his own* hurt, and changeth not.

P. He that putteth not out his money to usury, nor taketh reward against the innocent. He that doeth these *things* shall never be moved.

Evening.

Minister. HEAR the right, O Lord, attend unto my cry; give ear unto my prayer, *that goeth* not out of feigned lips.

People. Let my sentence come forth from thy presence; let thine eyes behold the things that are equal.

M. Thou hast proved mine heart; thou hast visited *me* in the night; thou hast tried me, *and* shalt find nothing: I am purposed *that* my mouth shall not transgress.

P. Concerning the works of men, by the word of thy lips I have kept *me from* the paths of the destroyer.

M. Hold up my goings in thy paths, *that* my footsteps slip not.

P. I have called upon thee, for thou wilt hear me, O God: incline thine ear unto me, *and* hear my speech.

M. Show thy marvellous lovingkindness, O thou that savest by thy right hand them which put their trust *in thee* from those that rise up *against them.*

P. Keep me as the apple of the eye; hide me under the shadow of thy wings,

From the wicked that oppress me,

from my deadly enemies, *who* compass me about.

M. They are inclosed in their own fat: with their mouth they speak proudly.

P. They have now compassed us in our steps: they have set their eyes bowing down to the earth;

M. Like as a lion *that* is greedy of his prey, and as it were a young lion lurking in secret places.

P. Arise, O Lord, disappoint him, cast him down: deliver my soul from the wicked, *which is* thy sword.

THIRTY-FIFTH SABBATH.

Morning.

Minister. THE Lord *is* in his holy temple, the Lord's throne *is* in heaven: his eyes behold, his eyelids try, the children of men.

People. Help, Lord; for the godly

man ceaseth; for the faithful fail from among the children of men.

M. They speak vanity every one with his neighbor: *with* flattering lips *and* with a double heart do they speak.

P. The Lord shall cut off all flattering lips, *and* the tongue that speaketh proud things:

Who have said, With our tongue will we prevail; our lips *are* our own: who *is* lord over us?

M. For the oppression of the poor, for the sighing of the needy, now will I arise, saith the Lord; I will set *him* in safety *from him that* puffeth at him.

P. The words of the Lord *are* pure words: *as* silver tried in a furnace of earth, purified seven times.

M. Thou shalt keep them, O Lord, thou shalt preserve them from this generation forever.

P. The wicked walk on every side, when the vilest men are exalted.

M. In the Lord put I my trust: how

say ye to my soul, Flee *as* a bird to your mountain?

P. For, lo, the wicked bend *their* bow, they make ready their arrow upon the string, that they may privily shoot at the upright in heart.

M. If the foundations be destroyed, what can the righteous do?

P. The LORD trieth the righteous: but the wicked and him that loveth violence his soul hateth.

M. Upon the wicked he shall rain snares, fire and brimstone, and a horrible tempest: *this shall be* the portion of their cup.

P. For the righteous LORD loveth righteousness; his countenance doth behold the upright.

Evening.

Minister. I WILL praise *thee*, O LORD, with my whole heart; I will show forth all thy marvellous works.

People. I will be glad and rejoice in thee: I will sing praise to thy name, O thou Most High.

M. When mine enemies are turned back, they shall fall and perish at thy presence.

P. But the LORD shall endure forever: he hath prepared his throne for judgment.

And he shall judge the world in righteousness, he shall minister judgment to the people in uprightness.

M. The LORD also will be a refuge for the oppressed, a refuge in times of trouble.

P. And they that know thy name will put their trust in thee: for thou, LORD, hast not forsaken them that seek thee.

M. Sing praises to the LORD, which dwelleth in Zion: declare among the people his doings.

P. When he maketh inquisition for blood, he remembereth them:

he forgetteth not the cry of the humble.

M. Have mercy upon me, O Lord; consider my trouble *which I suffer* of them that hate me, thou that liftest me up from the gates of death:

P. That I may show forth all thy praise in the gates of the daughter of Zion: I will rejoice in thy salvation.

M. The heathen are sunk down in the pit *that* they made: in the net which they hid is their own foot taken.

P. The Lord is known *by* the judgment *which* he executeth: the wicked is snared in the work of his own hands.

M. The wicked shall be turned into hell, *and* all the nations that forget God.

P. For the needy shall not always be forgotten: the expectation of the poor shall *not* perish forever.

THIRTY-SIXTH SABBATH.

Morning.

Minister. IN my distress I called upon the Lord, and cried unto my God: he heard my voice out of his temple, and my cry came before him, *even* into his ears.

People. Then the earth shook and trembled; the foundations also of the hills moved and were shaken, because he was wroth.

M. There went up a smoke out of his nostrils, and fire out of his mouth devoured: coals were kindled by it.

P. He bowed the heavens also, and came down: and darkness *was* under his feet.

M. And he rode upon a cherub, and did fly: yea, he did fly upon the wings of the wind.

P. He made darkness his secret place; his pavilion round about him *were* dark waters *and* thick clouds of the skies.

M. At the brightness *that was* before him his thick clouds passed, hail *stones* and coals of fire.

P. The LORD also thundered in the heavens, and the Highest gave his voice; hail *stones* and coals of fire.

M. Yea, he sent out his arrows, and scattered them; and he shot out lightnings, and discomfited them.

P. Then the channels of waters were seen, and the foundations of the world were discovered at thy rebuke, O LORD, at the blast of the breath of thy nostrils.

M. He sent from above, he took me, he drew me out of many waters.

P. He delivered me from my strong enemy, and from them which hated me: for they were too strong for me.

M. They prevented me in the day of my calamity: but the LORD was my stay.

P. He brought me forth also into

a large place; he delivered me, because he delighted in me.

Evening.

Minister. I WILL love thee, O LORD, my strength.

People. The LORD *is* my rock, and my fortress, and my deliverer; my God, my strength, in whom I will trust; my buckler, and the horn of my salvation, *and* my high tower.

M. I will call upon the LORD, *who is worthy* to be praised: so shall I be saved from mine enemies.

P. The sorrows of death compassed me, and the floods of ungodly men made me afraid.

M. The sorrows of hell compassed me about: the snares of death prevented me.

P. The LORD rewarded me according to my righteousness; according to the cleanness of my hands hath he recompensed me.

M. For I have kept the ways of the LORD, and have not wickedly departed from my God.

P. For all his judgments *were* before me, and I did not put away his statutes from me.

I was also upright before him, and I kept myself from mine iniquity.

M. Therefore hath the LORD recompensed me according to my righteousness, according to the cleanness of my hands in his eyesight.

P. With the merciful thou wilt show thyself merciful; with an upright man thou wilt show thyself upright;

M. With the pure thou wilt show thyself pure; and with the froward thou wilt show thyself froward.

For thou wilt save the afflicted people; but wilt bring down high looks.

P. For thou wilt light my candle: the LORD my God will enlighten my darkness.

M. For by thee I have run through

a troop; and by my God have I leaped over a wall.

P. As for God, his way *is* perfect: the word of the LORD is tried: he *is* a buckler to all those that trust in him.

THIRTY-SEVENTH SABBATH.

Morning.

Minister. THE LORD *is* my shepherd; I shall not want.

He maketh me to lie down in green pastures: he leadeth me beside the still waters.

People. He restoreth my soul: he leadeth me in the paths of righteousness for his name's sake.

M. Yea, though I walk through the valley of the shadow of death, I will fear no evil: for thou *art* with me; thy rod and thy staff they comfort me.

P. Thou preparest a table before-me

in the presence of mine enemies: thou anointest my head with oil; my cup runneth over.

M. Surely goodness and mercy shall follow me all the days of my life: and I will dwell in the house of the LORD forever.

P. The earth *is* the LORD's, and the fulness thereof; the world, and they that dwell therein.

For he hath founded it upon the seas, and established it upon the floods.

M. Who shall ascend into the hill of the LORD? and who shall stand in his holy place?

P. He that hath clean hands, and a pure heart; who hath not lifted up his soul unto vanity, nor sworn deceitfully.

M. He shall receive the blessing from the LORD, and righteousness from the God of his salvation.

P. This *is* the generation of them that seek him, that seek thy face, O Jacob.

M. Lift up your heads, O ye gates; and be ye lifted up, ye everlasting doors; and the King of glory shall come in.

P. Who *is* this King of glory? the LORD strong and mighty, the LORD mighty in battle.

M. Lift up your heads, O ye gates; even lift *them* up, ye everlasting doors; and the King of glory shall come in.

P. Who is this King of glory? the LORD of hosts, he *is* the King of glory.

Evening.

Minister. WHO *is* God save the LORD? or who *is* a rock save our God?

It is God that girdeth me with strength, and maketh my way perfect.

People. He maketh my feet like hinds' *feet*, and setteth me upon my high places.

He teacheth my hands to war, so that a bow of steel is broken by mine arms.

M. Thou hast also given me the shield of thy salvation: and thy right hand hath holden me up, and thy gentleness hath made me great.

P. Thou hast enlarged my steps under me, that my feet did not slip.

M. I have pursued mine enemies, and overtaken them: neither did I turn again till they were consumed.

P. I have wounded them that they were not able to rise: they are fallen under my feet.

M. For thou hast girded me with strength unto the battle: thou hast subdued under me those that rose up against me.

P. Thou hast delivered me from the strivings of the people; *and* thou hast made me the head of the heathen: a people *whom* I have not known shall serve me.

M. As soon as they hear of me, they shall obey me: the strangers shall submit themselves unto me.

The strangers shall fade away, and be afraid out of their close places.

P. The LORD liveth; and blessed *be* my Rock; and let the God of my salvation be exalted.

M. It is God that avengeth me, and subdueth the people under me.

P. He delivereth me from mine enemies: yea, thou liftest me up above those that rise up against me: thou hast delivered me from the violent man.

M. Therefore will I give thanks unto thee, O LORD, among the heathen, and sing praises unto thy name.

P. Great deliverance giveth he to his king; and showeth mercy to his anointed, to David, and to his seed for evermore.

THIRTY-EIGHTH SABBATH.

Morning.

Minister. ARISE, O God, plead thine own cause: remember how the foolish man reproacheth thee daily.

People. Forget not the voice of thine enemies: the tumult of those that rise up against thee increaseth continually.

M. In Judah *is* God known: his name *is* great in Israel.

P. In Salem also is his tabernacle, and his dwellingplace in Zion.

M. There brake he the arrows of the bow, the shield, and the sword, and the battle.

P. Thou *art* more glorious *and* excellent than the mountains of prey.

M. The stouthearted are spoiled, they have slept their sleep: and none of the men of might have found their hands.

P. At thy rebuke, O God of Jacob, both the chariot and horse are cast into a dead sleep.

M. Thou, *even* thou, *art* to be feared: and who may stand in thy sight when once thou art angry?

P. Thou didst cause judgment to be heard from heaven; the earth feared, and was still,

M. When God arose to judgment, to save all the meek of the earth.

P. Surely the wrath of man shall praise thee: the remainder of wrath shalt thou restrain.

M. Vow, and pay unto the Lord your God: let all that be round about him bring presents unto him that ought to be feared.

P. He shall cut off the spirit of princes: *he is* terrible to the kings of the earth.

Evening.

Minister. HOW long wilt thou forget me, O Lord? forever? how long wilt thou hide thy face from me?

People. The king shall joy in thy strength, O Lord; and in thy salvation how greatly shall he rejoice!

M. Thou hast given him his heart's desire, and hast not withholden the request of his lips.

P. For thou preventest him with the blessings of goodness: thou settest a crown of pure gold on his head.

M. He asked life of thee, *and* thou gavest *it* him, *even* length of days for ever and ever.

P. His glory *is* great in thy salvation: honor and majesty hast thou laid upon him.

M. For thou hast made him most blessed forever: thou hast made him exceeding glad with thy countenance.

P. For the king trusteth in the LORD, and through the mercy of the Most High he shall not be moved.

M. Thine hand shall find out all thine enemies: thy right hand shall find out those that hate thee.

P. Thou shalt make them as a fiery oven in the time of thine anger: the LORD shall swallow them up in his wrath, and the fire shall devour them.

M. Their fruit shalt thou destroy from the earth, and their seed from among the children of men.

P. For they intended evil against thee: they imagined a mischievous device, *which* they are not able *to perform.*

M. Therefore shalt thou make them turn their back, *when* thou shalt make ready *thine arrows* upon thy strings against the face of them.

P. Be thou exalted, LORD, in thine own strength: so will we sing and praise thy power.

THIRTY-NINTH SABBATH.

Morning.

Minister. TRULY God *is* good to Israel, *even* to such as are of a clean heart.

People. But as for me, my feet were almost gone; my steps had well nigh slipped.

For I was envious at the foolish, *when* I saw the prosperity of the wicked.

M. For *there are* no bands in their death: but their strength *is* firm.

They *are* not in trouble *as other* men; neither are they plagued like *other* men.

P. Therefore pride compasseth them about as a chain; violence covereth them *as* a garment.

Their eyes stand out with fatness: they have more than heart could wish.

M. They are corrupt, and speak

wickedly *concerning* oppression: they speak loftily.

They set their mouth against the heavens, and their tongue walketh through the earth.

P. Therefore his people return hither: and waters of a full *cup* are wrung out to them.

And they say, How doth God know? and is there knowledge in the Most High?

M. Behold, these *are* the ungodly, who prosper in the world; they increase *in* riches.

P. Verily I have cleansed my heart *in* vain, and washed my hands in innocency.

M. When I thought to know this, it *was* too painful for me;

Until I went into the sanctuary of God; *then* understood I their end.

P. Surely thou didst set them in slippery places: thou castedst them down into destruction.

How are they *brought* into desolation, as in a moment! they are utterly consumed with terrors.

M. Nevertheless I *am* continually with thee: thou hast holden *me* by my right hand.

P. Thou shalt guide me with thy counsel, and afterward receive me *to* glory.

M. Whom have I in heaven *but thee?* and *there is* none upon earth *that* I desire besides thee.

P. My flesh and my heart faileth: *but* God *is* the strength of my heart, and my portion forever.

Evening.

Minister. IN thee, O LORD, do I put my trust; let me never be ashamed: deliver me in thy righteousness.

People. Bow down thine ear to me; deliver me speedily: be thou my strong rock, for a house of defence to save me.

M. For thou *art* my rock and my fortress; therefore for thy name's sake lead me, and guide me.

P. Pull me out of the net that they have laid privily for me: for thou *art* my strength.

M. Into thine hand I commit my spirit: thou hast redeemed me, O Lord God of truth.

P. Have mercy upon me, O Lord, for I am in trouble: mine eye is consumed with grief, *yea,* my soul and my belly.

M. For my life is spent with grief, and my years with sighing: my strength faileth because of mine iniquity, and my bones are consumed.

P. I have heard the slander of many: fear *was* on every side: while they took counsel together against me, they devised to take away my life.

M. But I trusted in thee, O Lord: I said, Thou *art* my God.

My times *are* in thy hand: deliver

me from the hand of mine enemies, and from them that persecute me.

P. Make thy face to shine upon thy servant: save me for thy mercies' sake.

M. Let me not be ashamed, O LORD; for I have called upon thee: let the wicked be ashamed, *and* let them be silent in the grave.

Let the lying lips be put to silence; which speak grievous things proudly and contemptuously against the righteous.

P. Oh how great *is* thy goodness, which thou hast laid up for them that fear thee; *which* thou hast wrought for them that trust in thee before the sons of men!

M. Thou shalt hide them in the secret of thy presence from the pride of man: thou shalt keep them secretly in a pavilion from the strife of tongues.

P. Blessed *be* the LORD: for he hath showed me his marvellous kindness in a strong city.

FORTIETH SABBATH.

Morning.

Minister. PRAISE waiteth for thee, O God, in Zion: and unto thee shall the vow be performed.

People. O thou that hearest prayer, unto thee shall all flesh come.

M. Iniquities prevail against me: *as for* our transgressions, thou shalt purge them away.

P. Blessed *is the man whom* thou choosest, and causest to approach *unto thee, that* he may dwell in thy courts: we shall be satisfied with the goodness of thy house, *even* of thy holy temple.

M. By terrible things in righteousness wilt thou answer us, O God of our salvation; *who art* the confidence of all the ends of the earth, and of them that are afar off *upon* the sea:

P. Which by his strength setteth

fast the mountains; *being* girded with power:

M. Which stilleth the noise of the seas, the noise of their waves, and the tumult of the people.

P. They also that dwell in the uttermost parts are afraid at thy tokens: thou makest the outgoings of the morning and evening to rejoice.

M. Thou visitest the earth, and waterest it: thou greatly enrichest it with the river of God, *which* is full of water: thou preparest them corn, when thou hast so provided for it.

P. Thou waterest the ridges thereof abundantly: thou settlest the furrows thereof: thou makest it soft with showers: thou blessest the springing thereof.

M. Thou crownest the year with thy goodness; and thy paths drop fatness.

P. They drop *upon* the pastures of the wilderness: and the little hills rejoice on every side.

M. The pastures are clothed with flocks; the valleys also are covered over with corn; they shout for joy, they also sing.

P. Blessed *be* the Lord, *who* daily loadeth us *with benefits, even* the God of our salvation.

Evening.

Minister. I WILL give thee thanks in the great congregation: I will praise thee among much people.

People. Let not them that are mine enemies wrongfully rejoice over me: *neither* let them wink with the eye that hate me without a cause.

M. For they speak not peace: but they devise deceitful matters against *them that are* quiet in the land.

P. They rewarded me evil for good *to* the spoiling of my soul.

M. But as for me, when they were sick, my clothing *was* sackcloth: I humbled my soul with fasting; and my prayer returned into mine own bosom.

P. I behaved myself as though *he had been* my friend *or* brother: I bowed down heavily, as one that mourneth *for his* mother.

M. But in mine adversity they rejoiced, and gathered themselves together: *yea,* the abjects gathered themselves together against me, and I knew *it* not; they did tear *me,* and ceased not:

P. This thou hast seen, O Lord: keep not silence: O Lord, be not far from me.

M. Stir up thyself, and awake to my judgment, *even* unto my cause, my God and my Lord.

P. Judge me, O Lord my God, according to thy righteousness; and let them not rejoice over me.

M. Let them not say in their hearts, Ah, so would we have it: let them not say, We have swallowed him up.

P. Let them be ashamed and brought to confusion together that rejoice at mine hurt: let them be clothed with shame and dishonor that magnify *themselves* against me.

M. Let them shout for joy, and be glad, that favor my righteous cause: yea, let them say continually, Let the Lord be magnified, which hath pleasure in the prosperity of his servant.

P. And my tongue shall speak of thy righteousness *and* of thy praise all the day long.

FORTY-FIRST SABBATH.

Morning.

Minister. MY days *are* like a shadow that declineth; and I am withered like grass.

But thou, O Lord, shalt endure forever; and thy remembrance unto all generations.

People. Thou shalt arise, *and* have mercy upon Zion: for the time to favor her, yea, the set time, is come.

M. For thy servants take pleasure in her stones, and favor the dust thereof.

So the heathen shall fear the name of the Lord: and all the kings of the earth thy glory.

P. When the Lord shall build up Zion, he shall appear in his glory.

M. He will regard the prayer of the destitute, and not despise their prayer.

This shall be written for the generation to come: and the people which shall be created shall praise the Lord.

P. For he hath looked down from the height of his sanctuary; from heaven did the Lord behold the earth;

M. To hear the groaning of the prisoner; to loose those that are appointed to death;

To declare the name of the Lord in Zion, and his praise in Jerusalem;

P. When the people are gathered together, and the kingdoms, to serve the Lord.

M. He weakened my strength in the way; he shortened my days.

P. I said, O my God, take me not away in the midst of my days: thy years *are* throughout all generations.

M. Of old hast thou laid the foundation of the earth: and the heavens *are* the work of thy hands.

P. They shall perish, but thou shalt endure: yea, all of them shall wax old like a garment; as a vesture shalt thou change them, and they shall be changed:

M. But thou *art* the same, and thy years shall have no end.

P. The children of thy servants shall continue, and their seed shall be established before thee.

Evening.

Minister. MANY, O LORD my God, *are* thy wonderful works *which* thou hast done, and thy thoughts *which are* to us-ward :

People. They cannot be reckoned up in order unto thee : *if* I would declare and speak *of them*, they are more than can be numbered.

M. Sacrifice and offering thou didst not desire ; mine ears hast thou opened : burnt offering and sin offering hast thou not required.

P. Then said I, Lo, I come : in the volume of the book *it is* written of me,

M. I delight to do thy will, O my God : yea, thy law *is* within my heart.

P. I have preached righteousness in the great congregation : lo, I have not refrained my lips, O LORD, thou knowest.

M. I have not hid thy righteousness within my heart ; I have declared thy faithfulness and thy salvation: I have not concealed thy lovingkindness and thy truth from the great congregation.

P. Withhold not thou thy tender mercies from me, O LORD: let thy lovingkindness and thy truth continually preserve me.

M.. For innumerable evils have compassed me about: mine iniquities have taken hold upon me, so that I am not able to look up; they are more than the hairs of mine head: therefore my heart faileth me.

P. Be pleased, O LORD, to deliver me: O LORD, make haste to help me.

M. Let them be ashamed and confounded together that seek after my soul to destroy it; let them be driven backward and put to shame that wish me evil.

P. Let them be desolate for a reward of their shame that say unto me, Aha, aha.

M.. Let all those that seek thee rejoice and be glad in thee: let such as love thy salvation say continually, The LORD be magnified.

P. But I *am* poor and needy; *yet* the Lord thinketh upon me: thou *art* my help and my deliverer; make no tarrying, O my God.

FORTY-SECOND SABBATH.

Morning.

Minister. OH that *men* would praise the LORD *for* his goodness, and *for* his wonderful works to the children of men!

People. For he hath broken the gates of brass, and cut the bars of iron in sunder.

M. Fools, because of their transgression, and because of their iniquities are afflicted.

Their soul abhorreth all manner of

meat; and they draw near unto the gates of death.

P. Then they cry unto the Lord in their trouble, *and* he saveth them out of their distresses.

M. He sent his word, and healed them, and delivered *them* from their destructions.

P. Oh that *men* would praise the Lord *for* his goodness, and *for* his wonderful works to the children of men!

M. And let them sacrifice the sacrifices of thanksgiving, and declare his works with rejoicing.

P. They that go down to the sea in ships, that do business in great waters;

M. These see the works of the Lord, and his wonders in the deep.

For he commandeth, and raiseth the stormy wind, which lifteth up the waves thereof.

P. They mount up to the heaven,

they go down again to the depths: their soul is melted because of trouble.

M. They reel to and fro, and stagger like a drunken man, and are at their wit's end.

P. Then they cry unto the LORD in their trouble, and he bringeth them out of their distresses.

M. He maketh the storm a calm, so that the waves thereof are still.

Then are they glad because they be quiet; so he bringeth them unto their desired haven.

P. Oh that *men* would praise the LORD *for* his goodness, and *for* his wonderful works to the children of men!

Evening.

Minister. BE merciful unto me, O God: for man would swallow me up; he fighting daily oppresseth me.

People. Mine enemies would daily

swallow *me* up: for *they be* many that fight against me, O thou Most High.

What time I am afraid, I will trust in thee.

M. In God I will praise his word, in God I have put my trust; I will not fear what flesh can do unto me.

P. Every day they wrest my words: all their thoughts *are* against me for evil.

M. They gather themselves together, they hide themselves, they mark my steps, when they wait for my soul.

P. Shall they escape by iniquity? in *thine* anger cast down the people, O God.

M. How long shall I take counsel in my soul, *having* sorrow in my heart daily? how long shall mine enemy be exalted over me?

P. Consider *and* hear me, O Lord my God: lighten mine eyes, lest I sleep the *sleep of* death;

M. Lest mine enemy say, I have

prevailed against him; *and* those that trouble me rejoice when I am moved.

P. But I have trusted in thy mercy; my heart shall rejoice in thy salvation.

M. I will sing unto the Lord, because he hath dealt bountifully with me.

P. In God have I put my trust: I will not be afraid what man can do unto me.

M. Thy vows *are* upon me, O God: I will render praises unto thee.

P. For thou hast delivered my soul from death: *wilt* not *thou deliver* my feet from falling, that I may walk before God in the light of the living?

FORTY-THIRD SABBATH.

Morning.

Minister. BLESSED *be* the Lord my strength, which teacheth my hands to war, *and* my fingers to fight:

People. My goodness, and my fortress; my high tower, and my deliverer; my shield, and *he* in whom I trust; who subdueth my people under me.

M. LORD, what *is* man, that thou takest knowledge of him! *or* the son of man, that thou makest account of him!

P. Man is like to vanity: his days *are* as a shadow that passeth away.

M. Bow thy heavens, O LORD, and come down: touch the mountains, and they shall smoke.

Cast forth lightning, and scatter them: shoot out thine arrows, and destroy them.

P. Send thine hand from above; rid me, and deliver me out of great waters, from the hand of strange children;

M. Whose mouth speaketh vanity, and their right hand *is* a right hand of falsehood.

P. I will sing a new song unto thee, O God: upon a psaltery *and* an instrument of ten strings will I sing praises unto thee.

M. *It is he* that giveth salvation unto kings: who delivereth David his servant from the hurtful sword.

P. Rid me, and deliver me from the hand of strange children, whose mouth speaketh vanity, and their right hand *is* a right hand of falsehood:

M. That our sons *may be* as plants grown up in their youth; *that* our daughters *may be* as corner stones, polished *after* the similitude of a palace:

P. That our garners *may be* full, affording all manner of store; *that* our sheep may bring forth thousands and ten thousands in our streets:

M. That our oxen *may be* strong to labor; *that there be* no breaking in, nor going out; that *there be* no complaining in our streets.

P. Happy *is that* people, that is in such a case: *yea,* happy *is that* people, whose God *is* the Lord.

Evening.

Minister. HOW excellent *is* thy lovingkindness, O God! therefore the children of men put their trust under the shadow of thy wings.

People. They shall be abundantly satisfied with the fatness of thy house; and thou shalt make them drink of the river of thy pleasures.

M. For with thee *is* the fountain of life: in thy light shall we see light.

P. O continue thy lovingkindness unto them that know thee; and thy righteousness to the upright in heart.

M. Let not the foot of pride come against me, and let not the hand of the wicked remove me.

P. There are the workers of iniquity fallen: they are cast down, and shall not be able to rise.

M. Fret not thyself because of evil doers, neither be thou envious against the workers of iniquity.

P. For they shall soon be cut down like the grass, and wither as the green herb.

M. Trust in the LORD, and do good; *so* shalt thou dwell in the land, and verily thou shalt be fed.

P. Delight thyself also in the LORD; and he shall give thee the desires of thine heart.

M. Commit thy way unto the LORD; trust also in him; and he shall bring *it* to pass.

P. And he shall bring forth thy righteousness as the light, and thy judgment as the noonday.

M. Rest in the LORD, and wait patiently for him: fret not thyself because of him who prospereth in his way, because of the man who bringeth wicked devices to pass.

P. Cease from anger, and forsake

wrath: fret not thyself in any wise to do evil.

M. For evil doers shall be cut off: but those that wait upon the LORD, they shall inherit the earth.

FORTY-FOURTH SABBATH.

Morning.

Minister. LET God arise, let his enemies be scattered: let them also that hate him flee before him.

People. As smoke is driven away, *so* drive *them* away: as wax melteth before the fire, *so* let the wicked perish at the presence of God.

M. But let the righteous be glad; let them rejoice before God: yea, let them exceedingly rejoice.

P. Sing unto God, sing praises to his name: extol him that rideth upon the heavens by his name JAH, and rejoice before him.

M. A father of the fatherless, and a judge of the widows, *is* God in his holy habitation.

P. God setteth the solitary in families: he bringeth out those which are bound with chains: but the rebellious dwell in a dry *land.*

M. O God, when thou wentest forth before thy people, when thou didst march through the wilderness;

P. The earth shook, the heavens also dropped at the presence of God: *even* Sinai itself *was moved* at the presence of God, the God of Israel.

M. Thou, O God, didst send a plentiful rain, whereby thou didst confirm thine inheritance, when it was weary.

P. Thy congregation hath dwelt therein: thou, O God, hast prepared of thy goodness for the poor.

M. The Lord gave the word: great

was the company of those that published *it*.

P. The chariots of God *are* twenty thousand, *even* thousands of angels: the Lord *is* among them, *as in* Sinai, in the holy *place*.

M. Thou hast ascended on high, thou hast led captivity captive: thou hast received gifts for men; yea, *for* the rebellious also, that the LORD God might dwell *among them*.

Evening.

Minister. LORD, all my desire *is* before thee; and my groaning is not hid from thee.

People. My heart panteth, my strength faileth me: as for the light of mine eyes, it also is gone from me.

M. My lovers and my friends stand aloof from my sore; and my kinsmen stand afar off.

P. They also that seek after my life lay snares *for me;* and they that seek my hurt speak mischievous things, and imagine deceits all the day long.

M. But I, as a deaf *man,* heard not; and *I was* as a dumb man *that* openeth not his mouth.

P. Thus I was as a man that heareth not, and in whose mouth *are* no reproofs.

M. For in thee, O LORD, do I hope: thou wilt hear, O Lord my God.

P. For I said, *Hear me,* lest *otherwise* they should rejoice over me: when my foot slippeth, they magnify *themselves* against me.

M. For I *am* ready to halt, and my sorrow *is* continually before me.

P. For I will declare mine iniquity; I will be sorry for my sin.

M. But mine enemies *are* lively, *and* they are strong: and they that hate me wrongfully are multiplied.

P. They also that render evil for good are mine adversaries; because I follow *the thing that* good *is.*

M. Forsake me not, O LORD : O my God, be not far from me.

P. Make haste to help me, O Lord my salvation.

FORTY-FIFTH SABBATH.

Morning.

Minister. IT *is a* good *thing* to give thanks unto the LORD, and to sing praises unto thy name, O Most High.

People. To show forth thy lovingkindness in the morning, and thy faithfulness every night,

M. Upon an instrument of ten strings, and upon the psaltery; upon the harp with a solemn sound.

P. For thou, LORD, hast made me glad through thy work : I will triumph in the works of thy hands.

M. O LORD, how great are thy

works! *and* thy thoughts are very deep.

A brutish man knoweth not; neither doth a fool understand this.

P. When the wicked spring as the grass, and when all the workers of iniquity do flourish; *it is* that they shall be destroyed forever:

M. But thou, Lord, *art most* high for evermore.

For, lo, thine enemies, O Lord, for, lo, thine enemies shall perish; all the workers of iniquity shall be scattered.

P. But my horn shalt thou exalt like *the horn of* a unicorn: I shall be anointed with fresh oil.

M. Mine eye also shall see *my desire* on mine enemies, *and* mine ears shall hear *my desire* of the wicked that rise up against me.

P. The righteous shall flourish like the palm-tree: he shall grow like a cedar in Lebanon.

M. The Lord hath prepared his

throne in the heavens; and his kingdom ruleth over all.

P. Bless the LORD, ye his angels, that excel in strength, that do his commandments, hearkening unto the voice of his word.

M. Bless ye the LORD, all *ye* his hosts; *ye* ministers of his, that do his pleasure.

P. Bless the LORD, all his works in all places of his dominion: bless the LORD, O my soul.

Evening.

Minister. WE have heard with our ears, O God, our fathers have told us, *what* work thou didst in their days, in the times of old.

People. How thou didst drive out the heathen with thy hand, and plantedst them; *how* thou didst afflict the people, and cast them out.

M. For they got not the land in possession by their own sword, neither did their own arm save them: but thy right hand, and thine arm, and the light of thy countenance, because thou hadst a favor unto them.

P. Thou art my King, O God: command deliverances for Jacob.

M. Through thee will we push down our enemies: through thy name will we tread them under that rise up against us.

P. For I will not trust in my bow, neither shall my sword save me.

M. But thou hast saved us from our enemies, and hast put them to shame that hated us.

P. In God we boast all the day long, and praise thy name forever.

M. Our heart is not turned back, neither have our steps declined from thy way;

P. Though thou hast sore broken us in the place of dragons, and covered us with the shadow of death.

M. Awake, why sleepest thou, O Lord? arise, cast *us* not off forever.

P. Wherefore hidest thou thy face, *and* forgettest our affliction and our oppression?

M. For our soul is bowed down to the dust: our belly cleaveth unto the earth.

P. Arise for our help, and redeem us for thy mercies' sake.

FORTY-SIXTH SABBATH.

Morning.

Minister. O GOD, thou *art* my God; early will I seek thee: my soul thirsteth for thee, my flesh longeth for thee in a dry and thirsty land, where no water is;

People. To see thy power and thy glory, so *as* I have seen thee in the sanctuary.

M. Because thy lovingkindness *is* better than life, my lips shall praise thee.

P. Thus will I bless thee while I live: I will lift up my hands in thy name.

M. My soul shall be satisfied as *with* marrow and fatness; and my mouth shall praise *thee* with joyful lips:

P. When I remember thee upon my bed, *and* meditate on thee in the *night* watches.

M. Because thou hast been my help, therefore in the shadow of thy wings will I rejoice.

P. My soul followeth hard after thee: thy right hand upholdeth me.

M. I will go into thy house with burnt offerings: I will pay thee my vows,

P. Which my lips have uttered, and my mouth hath spoken, when I was in trouble.

M. I will offer unto thee burnt sacrifices of fatlings, with the incense of rams: I will offer bullocks with goats.

P. But verily God hath heard *me;* he hath attended to the voice of my prayer.

M. Blessed *be* God, which hath not turned away my prayer, nor his mercy from me.

Evening.

Minister. DELIVER me from mine enemies, O my God: defend me from them that rise up against me.

People. Deliver me from the workers of iniquity, and save me from bloody men.

M. For, lo, they lie in wait for my soul: the mighty are gathered against me; not *for* my transgression, nor *for* my sin, O LORD.

P. They run and prepare themselves without *my* fault: awake to help me, and behold.

M. Thou therefore, O Lord God of hosts, the God of Israel, awake to visit all the heathen : be not merciful to any wicked transgressors.

P. They return at evening : they make a noise like a dog, and go round about the city.

M. Behold, they belch out with their mouth : swords *are* in their lips : for who, *say they*, doth hear ?

P. But thou, O Lord, shalt laugh at them ; thou shalt have all the heathen in derision.

M. Because of his strength will I wait upon thee : for God *is* my defence.

P. The God of my mercy shall prevent me : God shall let me see *my desire* upon mine enemies.

M. Slay them not, lest my people forget : scatter them by thy power; and bring them down, O Lord our shield.

P. For the sin of their mouth *and* the words of their lips let them even be taken in their pride: and for cursing and lying *which* they speak.

M. But I will sing of thy power; yea, I will sing aloud of thy mercy in the morning: for thou hast been my defence and refuge in the day of my trouble.

P. Unto thee, O my strength, will I sing: for God *is* my defence, *and* the God of my mercy.

FORTY-SEVENTH SABBATH.

Morning.

Minister. I WILL bless the Lord at all times: his praise *shall* continually *be* in my mouth.

People. My soul shall make her boast in the Lord: the humble shall hear *thereof*, and be glad.

M. O magnify the Lord with me, and let us exalt his name together.

P. I sought the Lord, and he heard me, and delivered me from all my fears.

M. They looked unto him, and were lightened: and their faces were not ashamed.

P. This poor man cried, and the Lord heard *him*, and saved him out of all his troubles.

M. The angel of the Lord encampeth round about them that fear him, and delivereth them.

P. The Lord looketh from heaven; he beholdeth all the sons of men.

M. From the place of his habitation he looketh upon all the inhabitants of the earth.

P. He fashioneth their hearts alike; he considereth all their works.

M. There is no king saved by the multitude of a host: a mighty man is not delivered by much strength.

P. A horse *is* a vain thing for safety: neither shall he deliver *any* by his great strength.

P. My soul shall be joyful in the LORD: it shall rejoice in his salvation.

M. All my bones shall say, LORD, who *is* like unto thee, which deliverest the poor from him that is too strong for him, yea, the poor and the needy from him that spoileth him?

Evening.

Minister. IN thee, O LORD, do I put my trust: let me never be put to confusion.

Deliver me in thy righteousness, and cause me to escape: incline thine ear unto me, and save me.

People. Be thou my strong habitation, whereunto I may continually resort: thou hast given commandment to save me; for thou *art* my rock and my fortress.

M. Deliver me, O my God, out of the hand of the wicked, out of the hand of the unrighteous and cruel man.

P. For thou *art* my hope, O Lord

God: *thou art* my trust from my youth.

M. Let my mouth be filled *with* thy praise *and with* thy honor all the day.

P. Cast me not off in the time of old age; forsake me not when my strength faileth.

M. For mine enemies speak against me; and they that lay wait for my soul take counsel together,

P. Saying, God hath forsaken him: persecute and take him; for *there is* none to deliver *him*.

M. O God, be not far from me: O my God, make haste for my help.

P. My mouth shall show forth thy righteousness *and* thy salvation all the day; for I know not the numbers *thereof*.

M. I will go in the strength of the Lord God: I will make mention of thy righteousness, *even* of thine only.

P. O God, thou hast taught me from my youth: and hitherto have I declared thy wondrous works.

M. Now also when I am old and grayheaded, O God, forsake me not; until I have showed thy strength unto *this* generation, *and* thy power to every one *that* is to come.

P. Thy righteousness also, O God, *is* very high, who hast done great things: O God, who *is* like unto thee!

FORTY-EIGHTH SABBATH.

Morning.

Minister. GIVE unto the LORD, O ye mighty, give unto the LORD glory and strength.

People. Give unto the LORD the glory due unto his name; worship the LORD in the beauty of holiness.

M. The voice of the LORD *is* upon

the waters: the God of glory thundereth: the Lord *is* upon many waters.

P. The voice of the Lord *is* powerful; the voice of the Lord *is* full of majesty.

M. The voice of the Lord breaketh the cedars; yea, the Lord breaketh the cedars of Lebanon.

P. He maketh them also to skip like a calf; Lebanon and Sirion like a young unicorn.

M. The voice of the Lord divideth the flames of fire.

P. The voice of the Lord shaketh the wilderness; the Lord shaketh the wilderness of Kadesh.

M. The voice of the Lord maketh the hinds to calve, and discovereth the forests: and in his temple doth every one speak of *his* glory.

P. The Lord sitteth upon the flood; yea, the Lord sitteth King forever.

M. The Lord will give strength unto

his people; the Lord will bless his people with peace.

P. Sing unto the Lord, O ye saints of his, and give thanks at the remembrance of his holiness.

M. For his anger *endureth but* a moment; in his favor *is* life: weeping may endure for a night, but joy *cometh* in the morning.

P. To the end that *my* glory may sing praise to thee, and not be silent. O Lord my God, I will give thanks unto thee forever.

Evening.

Minister. I CRIED unto God with my voice, *even* unto God with my voice; and he gave ear unto me.

In the day of my trouble I sought the Lord: my soul refused to be comforted.

People. I remembered God, and was troubled: I complained, and my spirit was overwhelmed.

M. Thou holdest mine eyes waking: I am so troubled that I cannot speak.

I have considered the days of old, the years of ancient times.

P. I call to remembrance my song in the night: I commune with mine own heart: and my spirit made diligent search.

M. Will the Lord cast off forever? and will he be favorable no more?

Is his mercy clean gone forever? doth *his* promise fail for evermore?

P. Hath God forgotten to be gracious? hath he in anger shut up his tender mercies?

M. And I said, This *is* my infirmity: *but I will remember* the years of the right hand of the Most High.

P. I will remember the works of the LORD: surely I will remember thy wonders of old.

M. I will meditate also of all thy work, and talk of thy doings.

Thy way, O God, *is* in the sanctuary: who *is so* great a God as *our* God?

P. Thou *art* the God that doest wonders: thou hast declared thy strength among the people.

Thou hast with *thine* arm redeemed thy people, the sons of Jacob and Joseph.

M. The waters saw thee, O God, the waters saw thee; they were afraid: the depths also were troubled.

P. The clouds poured out water: the skies sent out a sound: thine arrows also went abroad.

M. The voice of thy thunder *was* in the heaven: the lightnings lightened the world: the earth trembled and shook.

P. Thy way *is* in the sea, and thy path in the great waters, and thy footsteps are not known.

FORTY-NINTH SABBATH.

Morning.

Minister. OH that *men* would praise the LORD *for* his goodness, and *for* his wonderful works to the children of men!

People. Let them exalt him also in the congregation of the people, and praise him in the assembly of the elders.

M. He turneth rivers into a wilderness, and the watersprings into dry ground;

P. A fruitful land into barrenness, for the wickedness of them that dwell therein.

M. He turneth the wilderness into a standing water, and dry ground into watersprings.

P. And there he maketh the hungry to dwell, that they may prepare a city for habitation;

M. And sow the fields, and plant vineyards, which may yield fruits of increase.

P. He blesseth them also, so that they are multiplied greatly; and suffereth not their cattle to decrease.

M. Again, they are minished and brought low through oppression, affliction, and sorrow.

P. He poureth contempt upon princes, and causeth them to wander in the wilderness, *where there is* no way.

M. Yet setteth he the poor on high from affliction, and maketh *him* families like a flock.

P. The righteous shall see *it*, and rejoice: and all iniquity shall stop her mouth.

M. The righteous shall be glad in the Lord, and shall trust in him; and all the upright in heart shall glory.

P. Whoso *is* wise, and will observe these *things*, even they shall understand the lovingkindness of the Lord.

Evening.

Minister. HE that dwelleth in the secret place of the Most High shall abide under the shadow of the Almighty.

People. I will say of the LORD, *He is* my refuge and my fortress: my God; in him will I trust.

M. Surely he shall deliver thee from the snare of the fowler, *and* from the noisome pestilence.

P. He shall cover thee with his feathers, and under his wings shalt thou trust: his truth *shall be thy* shield and buckler.

M. Thou shalt not be afraid for the terror by night; *nor* for the arrow *that* flieth by day;

P. Nor for the pestilence *that* walketh in darkness; *nor* for the destruction *that* wasteth at noonday.

M. A thousand shall fall at thy side, and ten thousand at thy right hand; *but* it shall not come nigh thee.

P. Only with thine eyes shalt thou behold and see the reward of the wicked.

Because thou hast made the Lord, *which is* my refuge, *even* the Most High, thy habitation;

M. There shall no evil befall thee, neither shall any plague come nigh thy dwelling.

For he shall give his angels charge over thee, to keep thee in all thy ways.

P. They shall bear thee up in *their* hands, lest thou dash thy foot against a stone.

M. Thou shalt tread upon the lion and adder: the young lion and the dragon shalt thou trample under feet.

P. Because he hath set his love upon me, therefore will I deliver him: I will set him on high, because he hath known my name.

M. He shall call upon me, and I will

answer him: I *will be* with him in trouble; I will deliver him, and honor him.

P. With long life will I satisfy him, and show him my salvation.

FIFTIETH SABBATH.

Morning.

Minister. OH give thanks unto the LORD, for *he is* good; for his mercy *endureth* forever.

People. Let the redeemed of the LORD say *so*, whom he hath redeemed from the hand of the enemy;

M. And gathered them out of the lands, from the east, and from the west, from the north, and from the south.

P. They wandered in the wilderness in a solitary way; they found no city to dwell in.

Hungry and thirsty, their soul fainted in them.

M. Then they cried unto the Lord in their trouble, *and* he delivered them out of their distresses.

P. And he led them forth by the right way, that they might go to a city of habitation.

M. Oh that *men* would praise the Lord *for* his goodness, and *for* his wonderful works to the children of men!

P. For he satisfieth the longing soul, and filleth the hungry soul with goodness.

M. Such as sit in darkness and in the shadow of death, *being* bound in affliction and iron;

P. Because they rebelled against the words of God, and contemned the counsel of the Most High:

M. Therefore he brought down their heart with labor;. they fell down, and *there was* none to help.

P. Then they cried unto the LORD in their trouble, *and* he saved them out of their distresses.

M. He brought them out of darkness and the shadow of death, and brake their bands in sunder.

P. Oh that *men* would praise the LORD *for* his goodness, and *for* his wonderful works to the children of men!

Evening.

Minister. LORD, thou hast been our dwellingplace in all generations.

People. Before the mountains were brought forth, or ever thou hadst formed the earth and the world, even from everlasting to everlasting, thou *art* God.

M. Thou turnest man to destruction; and sayest, Return, ye children of men.

For a thousand years in thy sight

are but as yesterday when it is past, and *as* a watch in the night.

P. Thou carriest them away as with a flood; they are *as* a sleep: in the morning *they are* like grass *which* groweth up.

M. In the morning it flourisheth, and groweth up; in the evening it is cut down, and withereth.

P. For we are consumed by thine anger, and by thy wrath are we troubled.

M. Thou hast set our iniquities before thee, our secret *sins* in the light of thy countenance.

For all our days are passed away in thy wrath; we spend our years as a tale *that is told*.

P. The days of our years *are* threescore years and ten; and if by reason of strength *they be* fourscore years, yet *is* their strength labor and sorrow; for it is soon cut off, and we fly away.

M. Who knoweth the power of thine anger? even according to thy fear, *so is* thy wrath.

P. So teach *us* to number our days, that we may apply *our* hearts unto wisdom.

M. Return, O Lord, how long? and let it repent thee concerning thy servants.

P. Oh satisfy us early with thy mercy; that we may rejoice and be glad all our days.

Make us glad according to the days *wherein* thou hast afflicted us, *and* the years *wherein* we have seen evil.

M. Let thy work appear unto thy servants, and thy glory unto their children.

P. And let the beauty of the Lord our God be upon us: and establish thou the work of our hands upon us; yea, the work of our hands establish thou it.

FIFTY-FIRST SABBATH.

Morning.

Minister. I LOVE the Lord, because he hath heard my voice *and* my supplications.

People. Because he hath inclined his ear unto me, therefore will I call upon *him* as long as I live.

M. The sorrows of death compassed me, and the pains of hell gat hold upon me: I found trouble and sorrow.

P. Then called I upon the name of the Lord; O Lord, I beseech thee, deliver my soul.

M. Gracious *is* the Lord, and righteous; yea, our God *is* merciful.

The Lord preserveth the simple: I was brought low, and he helped me.

P. Return unto thy rest, O my soul; for the Lord hath dealt bountifully with thee.

M. For thou hast delivered my soul

from death, mine eyes from tears, *and* my feet from falling.

P. I will walk before the Lord in the land of the living.

M. I believed, therefore have I spoken: I was greatly afflicted:

I said in my haste, All men *are* liars.

P. What shall I render unto the Lord *for* all his benefits toward me?

M. I will take the cup of salvation, and call upon the name of the Lord.

I will pay my vows unto the Lord now in the presence of all his people.

P. Precious in the sight of the Lord *is* the death of his saints.

O Lord, truly I *am* thy servant; I *am* thy servant, *and* the son of thy handmaid: thou hast loosed my bonds.

M. I will offer to thee the sacrifice of thanksgiving, and will call upon the name of the Lord.

I will pay my vows unto the Lord now in the presence of all his people,

P. In the courts of the LORD's house, in the midst of thee, O Jerusalem. Praise ye the LORD.

Evening.

Minister. BLESS the LORD, O my soul. O LORD my God, thou art very great; thou art clothed with honor and majesty:

People. Who coverest *thyself* with light as *with* a garment: who stretchest out the heavens like a curtain:

M. Who layeth the beams of his chambers in the waters: who maketh the clouds his chariot: who walketh upon the wings of the wind:

P. Who maketh his angels spirits; his ministers a flaming fire:

M. Who laid the foundations of the earth, *that* it should not be removed forever.

Thou coveredst it with the deep as *with* a garment: the waters stood above the mountains.

P. He sendeth the springs into the valleys, *which* run among the hills.

They give drink to every beast of the field: the wild asses quench their thirst.

M. By them shall the fowls of the heaven have their habitation, *which* sing among the branches.

P. The trees of the Lord are full *of sap;* the cedars of Lebanon, which he hath planted;

M. Where the birds make their nests: *as for* the stork, the fir trees *are* her house.

The high hills *are* a refuge for the wild goats; *and* the rocks for the conies.

P. He appointed the moon for seasons: the sun knoweth his going down.

M. Thou makest darkness, and it is night: wherein all the beasts of the forest do creep *forth.*

P. The young lions roar after their prey, and seek their meat from God.

M. The sun ariseth, they gather themselves together, and lay them down in their dens.

P. Man goeth forth unto his work and to his labor until the evening.

M. O LORD, how manifold are thy works! in wisdom hast thou made them all: the earth is full of thy riches.

FIFTY-SECOND SABBATH.

Morning.

Minister. PRAISE ye the LORD. I will praise the LORD with *my* whole heart, in the assembly of the upright, and *in* the congregation.

People. The works of the LORD *are* great, sought out of all them that have pleasure therein.

M. His work *is* honorable and glorious: and his righteousness endureth forever.

P. He hath made his wonderful works to be remembered : the Lord *is* gracious and full of compassion.

M. He hath given meat unto them that fear him : he will ever be mindful of his covenant.

P. Praise the Lord, O Jerusalem; praise thy God, O Zion.

M. For he hath strengthened the bars of thy gates; he hath blessed thy children within thee.

P. He maketh peace *in* thy borders, *and* filleth thee with the finest of the wheat.

M. He sendeth forth his commandment *upon* earth : his word runneth very swiftly.

P. He giveth snow like wool : he scattereth the hoar frost like ashes.

M. He casteth forth his ice like morsels : who can stand before his cold?

P. He sendeth out his word, and melteth them : he causeth his wind to blow, *and* the waters flow.

M. He showeth his word unto Jacob, his statutes and his judgments unto Israel.

P. He hath not dealt so with any nation: and *as for his* judgments, they have not known them. Praise ye the Lord.

Evening.

Minister. RETURN, O Lord, deliver my soul: oh save me for thy mercies' sake.

People. For in death *there is* no remembrance of thee: in the grave who shall give thee thanks?

M. But the Lord shall endure for ever: he hath prepared his throne for judgment.

P. And he shall judge the world in righteousness, he shall minister judgment to the people in uprightness.

M. Lord, make me to know mine end, and the measure of my days, what it *is;* *that* I may know how frail I *am.*

P. Behold, thou hast made my days *as* a handbreadth; and mine age *is* as nothing before thee: verily every man at his best state *is* altogether vanity.

M. Surely every man walketh in a vain show: surely they are disquieted in vain: he heapeth up *riches*, and knoweth not who shall gather them.

P. And now, Lord, what wait I for? my hope *is* in thee.

M. Deliver me from all my transgressions: make me not the reproach of the foolish.

P. I was dumb, I opened not my mouth; because thou didst *it*.

M. Remove thy stroke away from me: I am consumed by the blow of thine hand.

P. When thou with rebukes dost correct man for iniquity, thou makest his beauty to consume away like a moth: surely every man *is* vanity.

M. Hear my prayer, O Lord, and give ear unto my cry; hold not thy peace at my tears: for I *am* a stranger with thee, *and* a sojourner, as all my fathers *were*.

P. Oh spare me, that I may recover strength, before I go hence, and be no more.

FIFTY-THIRD SABBATH.*

Morning.

Minister. PRAISE ye the Lord. Oh give thanks unto the Lord; for *he is* good: for his mercy *endureth* for ever.

People. Who can utter the mighty acts of the Lord? *who* can show forth all his praise?

Blessed *are* they that keep judgment, *and* he that doeth righteousness at all times.

M. Remember me, O Lord, with the

---

* This selection will only be needed every fourth year. It will be found appropriate, however, for Thanksgiving day, or any other special service.

favour *that thou bearest unto* thy people: Oh visit me with thy salvation;

That I may see the good of thy chosen, that I may rejoice in the gladness of thy nation, that I may glory with thine inheritance.

P. We have sinned with our fathers, we have committed iniquity, we have done wickedly.

M. Our fathers understood not thy wonders in Egypt; they remembered not the multitude of thy mercies; but provoked *him* at the sea, *even* at the Red sea.

P. Nevertheless he saved them for his name's sake, that he might make his mighty power to be known.

M. He rebuked the Red sea also, and it was dried up: so he led them through the depths, as through the wilderness.

P. And he saved them from the hand of him that hated *them*, and redeemed them from the hand of the enemy.

M. And the waters covered their enemies: there was not one of them left.

Then believed they his words; they sang his praise.

P. Many times did he deliver them; but they provoked *him* with their counsel, and were brought low for their iniquity.

M. Nevertheless he regarded their affliction, when he heard their cry:

And he remembered for them his covenant, and repented according to the multitude of his mercies.

P. He made them also to be pitied of all those that carried them captives.

M. Save us, O Lord our God, and gather us from among the heathen, to give thanks unto thy holy name, *and* to triumph in thy praise.

P. Blessed *be* the Lord God of Israel from everlasting to everlasting: and let all the people say, Amen. Praise ye the Lord.

Evening.

Minister. THE LORD *is* my strength and song, and is become my salvation.

People. The voice of rejoicing and salvation *is* in the tabernacles of the righteous: the right hand of the LORD doeth valiantly.

M. The right hand of the LORD is exalted: the right hand of the LORD doeth valiantly.

P. I shall not die, but live, and declare the works of the LORD.

M. The LORD hath chastened me sore: but he hath not given me over unto death.

P. Open to me the gates of righteousness: I will go into them, *and* I will praise the LORD:

M. This gate of the LORD, into which the righteous shall enter.

P. I will praise thee: for thou hast heard me, and art become my salvation.

M. The stone *which* the builders refused is become the head *stone* of the corner.

This is the Lord's doing; it *is* marvellous in our eyes.

P. Make a joyful noise unto the Lord, all the earth: make a loud noise and rejoice, and sing praise.

M. Sing unto the Lord with the harp; with the harp, and the voice of a psalm.

With trumpets and sound of cornet make a joyful noise before the Lord, the King.

P. Let the sea roar, and the fulness thereof; the world, and they that dwell therein.

M. Let the floods clap *their* hands: let the hills be joyful together

P. Before the Lord; for he cometh to judge the earth: with righteousness shall he judge the world, and the people with equity.

THE LORD'S PRAYER.

OUR Father who art in heaven, hallowed be thy name. Thy kingdom come. Thy will be done in earth, as it is in heaven. Give us this day our daily bread; and forgive us our trespasses, as we forgive them that trespass against us; and lead us not into temptation, but deliver us from evil; for thine is the kingdom, and the power, and the glory, forever. *Amen.*

THE TEN COMMANDMENTS.

1.

THOU shalt have no other gods before me.

2.

Thou shalt not make unto thee any graven image, or any likeness *of any thing* that *is* in heaven above, or that *is* in the earth beneath, or that *is* in the water under the earth: thou shalt not bow down thyself to them, nor serve them: for I the Lord thy God *am* a jealous God, visiting the iniquity of the fathers upon the children unto the third and fourth *generation* of them that hate me; and showing mercy unto thousands of them that love me, and keep my commandments.

3.

Thou shalt not take the name of the Lord thy God in vain: for the Lord will not hold him guiltless that taketh his name in vain.

4.

Remember the sabbath day, to keep it holy. Six days shalt thou labor, and do all thy work: but the seventh day *is* the sabbath of the Lord thy God: *in it* thou shalt not do any work, thou, nor thy son, nor thy daughter, thy manservant, nor thy maidservant, nor thy cattle, nor thy stranger that *is* within thy gates: for *in* six days the Lord made heaven and earth, the sea, and all that in them *is*, and rested the seventh day: wherefore the Lord blessed the sabbath day, and hallowed it.

5.

Honor thy father and thy mother: that thy days may be long upon the land which the Lord thy God giveth thee.

6.

Thou shalt not kill.

7.

Thou shalt not commit adultery.

8.

Thou shalt not steal.

9.

Thou shalt not bear false witness against thy neighbor.

10.

Thou shalt not covet thy neighbor's house, thou shalt not covet thy neighbor's wife, nor his manservant, nor his maidservant, nor his ox, nor his ass, nor any thing that *is* thy neighbor's.

THE APOSTLES' CREED.

I BELIEVE in God the Father Almighty, maker of heaven and earth: and in Jesus Christ his only Son our Lord; who was conceived by the Holy Ghost, born of the Virgin Mary; suffered under Pontius Pilate, was crucified, dead, and buried; the third day he rose from the dead; he ascended into heaven, and sitteth on the right hand of God the Father Almighty; from thence he shall come to judge the quick and the dead.

I believe in the Holy Ghost; the holy Catholic Church; the communion of saints; the forgiveness of sins; the resurrection of the body; and the life everlasting. Amen.

SELECTIONS

FROM THE

RITUAL.

MINISTRATION OF BAPTISM.

RECEIVING PERSONS INTO THE CHURCH AFTER PROBATION.

THE LORD'S SUPPER.

THE MINISTRATION

OF

BAPTISM TO INFANTS.

The Minister, coming to the Font, which is to be filled with pure Water, shall use the following:

DEARLY beloved, forasmuch as all men are conceived and born in sin, and that our Saviour Christ saith, Except a man be born of water, and of the Spirit, he cannot enter into the kingdom of God; I beseech you to call upon God the Father, through our Lord Jesus Christ, that having, of his bounteous mercy, redeemed *this child* by the blood of His Son, He will grant that *he*, being baptized with water, may also be baptized with the Holy Ghost, be received into Christ's holy Church, and become *a lively member* of the same.

Then shall the Minister say,

Let us pray.

ALMIGHTY and everlasting God, who of thy great mercy hast condescended to enter into covenant relations with man, wherein thou hast included children as partakers of its gracious benefits, declaring that of such is thy kingdom; and in thy ancient Church didst appoint divers baptisms, figuring thereby the renewing of the Holy Ghost; and by thy well-beloved Son Jesus Christ gavest commandment to thy holy apostles to go into all the world and disciple all nations, baptizing them in the name of the Father, and of the Son, and of the Holy Ghost: We beseech thee, that of thine infinite mercy thou wilt look upon *this child:* wash *him* and sanctify *him;* that *he,* being saved by thy grace, may be received into Christ's holy Church, and being steadfast in faith, joyful through hope, and rooted in love, may so overcome the evils of this present world, that finally *he* may attain to everlasting life, and reign with thee, world without end, through Jesus Christ our Lord. *Amen.*

O merciful God, grant that all carnal affections may die in *him,* and that all things belonging to the Spirit may live and grow in *him. Amen.*

Grant that *he* may have power and strength to have victory, and to triumph against the devil, the world, and the flesh. *Amen.*

Grant that whosoever is dedicated to thee by our office and ministry may also be endued with heavenly virtues, and everlastingly rewarded through thy mercy, O blessed Lord God, who dost live and govern all things, world without end. *Amen.*

Almighty, ever-living God, whose most dearly beloved Son Jesus Christ, for the forgiveness of our sins, did shed out of His most precious side both water and blood, regard, we beseech thee, our supplications. Sanctify this water for this holy sacrament; and grant that *this child,* now to be baptized, may receive the fullness of thy grace, and ever remain in the number of thy faithful and elect children, through Jesus Christ our Lord. *Amen.*

Then shall the Minister address the parents [or guardians] as follows:

DEARLY beloved; Forasmuch as *this child is* now presented by you for Christian baptism, *you* must remember that it is your part and duty to see that *he* be taught, as soon as *he* shall be able to learn, the nature and end of this holy sacrament. And that *he* may know these things the better, *you* shall call upon *him* to give reverent attendance upon the appointed means of grace, such as the ministry of the word and the public and private worship of God; and further, ye shall provide that *he* shall read the Holy Scriptures, and learn the Lord's Prayer, the Ten Commandments, the Apostles' Creed, the Catechism, and all other things which a Christian ought to know and believe to *his* soul's health, in order that *he* may be brought up to lead a virtuous and holy life, remembering always that baptism doth represent unto us that inward purity which disposeth us to follow the example of our Saviour

Christ; that as he died and rose again for us, so should we, who are baptized, die unto sin and rise again unto righteousness, continually mortifying all corrupt affections, and daily proceeding in all virtue and godliness.

Do *you* therefore solemnly engage to fulfill these duties, so far as in you lies, the Lord being your helper?

Answ. We do.

Then shall the people stand up, and the Minister shall say:.

Hear the words of the Gospel, written by St. Mark; [Ch. X, ver. 13–16.]

THEY brought young children to Christ, that he should touch them. And his disciples rebuked those that brought them; but when Jesus saw it, he was much displeased, and said unto them, Suffer the little children to come unto me, and forbid them not, for of such is the kingdom of God. Verily I say unto you, Whosoever shall not receive the kingdom of God as a little child he shall not enter therein. And he took them up in his arms, put his hands upon them, and blessed them.

Then the Minister shall take the Child into his hands, and say to the friends of the child,

Name this child.

And then, naming it after them, he shall sprinkle or pour Water upon it, or, if desired, immerse it in Water, saying,

N., I baptize thee in the name of the Father, and of the Son, and of the Holy Ghost. Amen.

Then shall the Minister offer the following prayer, the people kneeling:

O GOD of infinite mercy, the Father of all the faithful seed, be pleased to grant unto this child an understanding mind and a sanctified heart. May thy providence lead *him* through the dangers, temptations, and ignorance of *his* youth, that *he* may never run into folly nor into the evils of an unbridled appetite. We pray thee so to order the course of *his* life, that by good education, by holy examples, and by thy restraining and renewing grace, *he* may be led to serve thee faithfully all *his* days, so that, when *he* has glorified thee in *his* generation, and has served the Church on earth, *he* may be received into thine eternal kingdom, through Jesus Christ our Lord. *Amen.*

Almighty and most merciful Father, let thy loving mercy and compassion descend upon these, thy servant and handmaid, the parents [or guardians] of this child. Grant unto them, we beseech thee, thy Holy Spirit, that they may, like Abraham, command their household to keep the way of the Lord. Direct their actions and sanctify their hearts, words, and purposes, that their whole family may be united to our Lord Jesus Christ in the bands of faith, obedience, and charity; and that they all, being in this life thy holy children by adoption and grace, may be admitted into the Church of the first-born in heaven, through the merits of thy dear Son, our Saviour and Redeemer. *Amen.*

Then may the Minister offer extemporary prayer.

Then shall be said, all kneeling,

OUR Father who art in heaven, hallowed be thy name. Thy kingdom come. Thy will be done in earth, as it is in heaven. Give us this day our daily bread; and forgive us our trespasses, as we forgive them that trespass against us; and lead us not into temptation, but deliver us from evil; for thine is the kingdom, and the power, and the glory, forever. *Amen.*

THE

MINISTRATION OF BAPTISM

TO SUCH AS ARE OF RIPER YEARS.

DEARLY beloved, forasmuch as all men are conceived and born in sin; and that which is born of the flesh is flesh, and they that are in the flesh cannot please God, but live in sin, committing many actual transgressions; and our Saviour Christ saith, Except a man be born of water, and of the Spirit, he cannot enter into the kingdom of God:—I beseech you to call upon God the Father, through our Lord Jesus Christ, that of His bounteous goodness

He will grant to *these persons* that which by nature *they* cannot have; that *they*, being baptized with water, may also be baptized with the Holy Ghost, and being received into Christ's holy Church may continue lively *members* of the same.

Then shall the Minister say,

Let us pray.

ALMIGHTY and immortal God, the aid of all that need, the helper of all that flee to thee for succour, the life of them that believe, and the resurrection of the dead: we call upon thee for *these persons;* that *they*, coming to thy holy baptism, may also be filled with thy Holy Spirit. Receive *them*, O Lord, as thou hast promised by thy well-beloved Son, saying, Ask, and ye shall receive; seek, and ye shall find;

BAPTISM OF ADULTS.

knock, and it shall be opened unto you: so give now unto us that ask: let us that seek, find: open the gate unto us that knock; that *these persons* may enjoy the everlasting benediction of thy heavenly washing, and may come to the eternal kingdom which thou hast promised by Christ our Lord. *Amen.*

Then shall the people stand up; and the Minister shall say,

Hear the words of the Gospel writ ten by St. John, [Ch. III, ver. 1–8.]

THERE was a man of the Pharisees, named Nicodemus, a ruler of the Jews; the same came to Jesus by night, and said unto him, Rabbi, we know that thou art a teacher come from God; for no man can do these miracles that thou doest except God be with him. Jesus answered and said unto him, Verily, verily, I say unto thee, Except a man be born again, he cannot see the kingdom of God. Nicodemus saith unto him, How can a man be born when he is old? Can he enter the second time into his mother's womb, and be born? Jesus answered, Verily, verily, I say unto thee, Except a man be born of water and of the Spirit, he cannot enter into the kingdom of God. That which is born of the flesh is flesh, and that which is born of the Spirit is spirit. Marvel not that I said unto thee, Ye must be born again. The wind bloweth where it listeth, and thou hearest the sound thereof; but canst not tell whence it cometh, and whither it goeth: so is every one that is born of the Spirit.

Then the Minister shall speak to the persons to be baptized on this wise:

WELL beloved, who *have* come hither, desiring to receive holy baptism, you have heard how the congregation hath prayed, that our Lord Jesus Christ would vouchsafe to receive you, to bless you, and to give you the kingdom of heaven, and everlasting life. And our Lord Jesus Christ hath promised in His holy word to grant all those things that we have prayed for: which promise He for His part will most surely keep and perform.

Wherefore after this promise made by Christ, *you* must also faithfully, for *your* part, promise, in the presence of this whole congregation, that you will renounce the devil and all his works, and constantly believe God's holy word, and obediently keep His commandments.

Then shall the Minister demand of each of the persons to be baptized,

Quest. DOST thou renounce the devil and all his works, the vain pomp and glory of the world, with all covetous desires of the same, and the carnal desires of the flesh, so that thou wilt not follow or be led by them.

Answ. I renounce them all.

Quest. Dost thou believe in God the Father Almighty, Maker of heaven and earth? and in Jesus Christ His only-begotten Son our Lord? and that He was conceived by the Holy Ghost, born of the Virgin Mary? that He suffered under Pontius Pilate, was crucified, dead and buried: that He rose again the third day; that He ascended into heaven, and sitteth at the right hand of God the Father Almighty, and from thence shall come again at the end of the world, to judge the quick and the dead?

And dost thou believe in the Holy Ghost, the holy Catholic Church,* the communion of saints; the remission of sins; the resurrection of the body, and everlasting life after death?

Answ. All this I steadfastly believe.

Quest. Wilt thou be baptized in this faith?

Answ. This is my desire.

Quest. Wilt thou then obediently keep God's holy will and commandments, and walk in the same all the days of thy life?

Answ. I will endeavor so to do, God being my helper.

Then shall the Minister say,

O MERCIFUL GOD, grant that all carnal affections may die in these

* The one universal Church of Christ.

persons, and that all things belonging to the Spirit may live and grow in *them. Amen.*

Grant that *they* may have power and strength to have victory, and triumph against the devil, the world, and the flesh. *Amen.*

Grant that *they*, being here dedicated to thee by our office and ministry, may also be endued with heavenly virtues, and everlastingly rewarded, through thy mercy, O blessed Lord God, who dost live and govern all things, world without end. *Amen.*

Almighty, ever-living God, whose most dearly beloved Son Jesus Christ, for the forgiveness of our sins, did shed out of His most precious side both water and blood; and gave commandment to His disciples, that they should go teach all nations, and baptize them in the name of the Father, and of the

Son, and of the Holy Ghost: regard, we beseech thee, our supplications; and grant that the *persons* now to be baptized may receive the fullness of thy grace, and ever remain in the number of thy faithful and elect children, through Jesus Christ our Lord. *Amen.*

Then shall the Minister ask the name of each person to be baptized, and shall sprinkle or pour water upon him, (or, if he shall desire it, shall immerse him in water,) saying,

N., I baptize thee in the name of the Father, and of the Son, and of the Holy Ghost. *Amen.*

Then shall be said the Lord's prayer, all kneeling.

OUR Father who art in heaven, hallowed be thy name. Thy kingdom come. Thy will be done in earth, as it is in heaven. Give us this day our daily bread; and forgive us our trespasses, as we forgive them that trespass against us: and lead us not into temptation; but deliver us from evil: for thine is the kingdom, and the power, and the glory, forever. *Amen.*

Then may the Minister conclude with extemporary prayer.

FORM

FOR

RECEIVING PERSONS INTO THE CHURCH AFTER PROBATION.

Upon the day appointed, all that are to be received shall be called forward, and the Minister, addressing the congregation, shall say,

DEARLY BELOVED BRETHREN: The Scriptures teach us that the Church is the household of God, the body of which Christ is the Head, and that it is the design of the Gospel to bring together in one all who are in Christ. The fellowship of the Church is the communion that its members enjoy, one with another. The ends of this fellowship are, the maintenance of sound doctrine, and of the ordinances of Christian worship, and the exercise of that power of godly admonition and discipline which Christ has committed to his Church for the promotion of holiness. It is the duty of all men to unite in this fellowship, for it is only those that "be planted in the house of the Lord, that shall flourish in the courts of our God." Its more particular *duties* are, to promote peace and unity; to bear one another's burdens; to prevent each other's stumbling; to seek the intimacy of friendly society among themselves; to continue steadfast in the faith and worship of the Gospel; and to pray and sympathize with each other. Among its *privileges* are, peculiar incitements to holiness from the hearing of God's word and sharing in Christ's ordinances; the being placed under the watchful care of pastors, and the enjoyment of the blessings which are promised only to those who are of the household of faith. Into this holy fellowship the persons before you, who have already received the sacrament of baptism and have been under the care of proper leaders for six months on trial, come seeking admission. We now propose, in the fear of God, to question them as to their faith and purposes, that you may know that they are proper persons to be admitted into the Church.

Then addressing the applicants for admission, the Minister shall say:

DEARLY BELOVED: You are come hither seeking the great privilege of union with the Church our Saviour has purchased with his own blood. We rejoice in the grace of God vouchsafed unto you in that He has called you to be His *followers*, and that thus far you have run well. You have heard how blessed are the privileges and how solemn are the duties of membership in Christ's Church; and before you are fully admitted thereto, it is proper that you do here publicly renew your vows, confess your faith, and declare your purpose, by answering the following questions:

Do you here, in the presence of God and of this congregation, renew the solemn promise contained in the baptismal covenant, ratifying and confirming the same, and acknowledging yourselves bound faithfully to observe and keep that covenant?

Answ. I do.

Have you saving faith in the Lord Jesus Christ?

Answ. I trust I have.

Do you believe in the doctrines of

Holy Scripture, as set forth in the Articles of Religion of the Methodist Episcopal Church?

Answ. I do.

Will you cheerfully be governed by the rules of the Methodist Episcopal Church, hold sacred the ordinances of God, and endeavor, as much as in you lies, to promote the welfare of your brethren and the advancement of the Redeemer's kingdom?

Answ. I will.

Will you contribute of your earthly substance, according to your ability, to the support of the Gospel, and the various benevolent enterprises of the Church?

Answ. I will.

Then the Minister, addressing the Church, shall say:

BRETHREN, you have heard the responses given to our inquiries.

Have any of you reason to allege why these persons should not be received into full membership in the Church?

No objection being alleged, the Minister shall say to the candidates:

WE welcome you to the communion of the Church of God; and in testimony of our Christian affection and the cordiality with which we receive you, I hereby extend to you the right hand of fellowship; and may God grant that you may be *a* faithful and useful *member* of the Church militant till you are called to the fellowship of the Church triumphant, which is "without fault before the throne of God."

Then shall the Minister offer extemporary prayer.

THE ORDER FOR THE ADMINISTRATION

OF

THE LORD'S SUPPER.

The Elder shall say one or more of these sentences, during the reading of which, the persons appointed for that purpose shall receive the alms for the poor:

LET your light so shine before men, that they may see your good works, and glorify your Father which is in heaven. [Matt. v, 16.]

Lay not up for yourselves treasures upon earth, where moth and rust doth corrupt, and where thieves break through and steal: but lay up for yourselves treasures in heaven, where neither moth nor rust doth corrupt, and where thieves do not break through nor steal. [Matt. vi, 19, 20.]

Whatsoever ye would that men should do to you, do ye even so to them: for this is the law and the prophets. [Matt. vii, 12.]

Not every one that saith unto me, Lord, Lord, shall enter into the kingdom of heaven; but he that doeth the will of my Father which is in heaven. [Matt. vii, 21.]

Zaccheus stood, and said unto the Lord, Behold, Lord, the half of my goods I give to the poor; and if I have taken anything from any man, by false accusation, I restore him fourfold. [Luke xix, 8.]

He which soweth sparingly shall reap also sparingly; and he which soweth bountifully shall reap also bountifully. Every man according as he purposeth in his heart, so let him give; not grudgingly, or of necessity: for God loveth a cheerful giver. [2 Cor. ix, 6, 7.]

As we have therefore opportunity, let us do good unto all men, especially unto them who are of the household of faith. [Gal. vi, 10.]

Godliness with contentment is great gain; for we brought nothing into this world, and it is certain we can carry nothing out. [1 Tim. vi, 6, 7.]

Charge them that are rich in this world, that they be not high-minded, nor trust in uncertain riches, but in the living God, who giveth us richly all things to enjoy; that they do good, that they be rich in good works, ready to distribute, willing to communicate; laying up in store for themselves a good foundation against the time to come, that they may lay hold on eternal life. [1 Tim. vi, 17–19.]

God is not unrighteous to forget your work and labor of love, which ye have showed toward his name, in that ye have ministered to the saints and do minister. [Heb. vi, 10.]

To do good, and to communicate, forget not; for with such sacrifices God is well pleased. [Heb. xiii, 16.]

Whoso hath this world's good, and seeth his brother have need, and shutteth up his bowels of compassion from him, how dwelleth the love of God in him? [1 John iii, 17.]

He that hath pity upon the poor, lendeth unto the Lord; and that which he hath given will he pay him again. [Prov. xix, 17.]

Blessed is he that considereth the poor; the Lord will deliver him in time of trouble. [Psalm xli, 1.]

After which the Elder shall give the following Invitation, *the people standing:*

IF any man sin, we have an advocate with the Father, Jesus Christ the righteous: and he is the propitiation for our sins: and not for ours only, but also for the sins of the whole world.

Wherefore, ye that do truly and earnestly repent of your sins, and are in love and charity with your neighbors, and intend to lead a new life, following the commandments of God, and walking from henceforth in His holy ways; draw near with faith, and take this holy sacrament to your comfort: and, devoutly kneeling, make your humble confession to Almighty God.

Then shall this general confession be made by the Minister in the name of all those who are minded to receive the holy communion, both he and all the people devoutly kneeling, and saying:

ALMIGHTY God, Father of our Lord Jesus Christ, Maker of all things, Judge of all men: we acknowledge and bewail our manifold sins and wickedness, which we from time to time most grievously have committed, by thought, word, and deed, against thy Divine Majesty, provoking most justly thy wrath and indignation against us. We do earnestly repent, and are heartily sorry for these our misdoings; the remembrance of them is grievous unto us. Have mercy upon us, have mercy upon us, most merciful Father; for thy Son, our Lord Jesus Christ's sake, forgive us all that is past; and grant that we may ever hereafter serve and please thee in newness of life, to the honor and glory of thy name, through Jesus Christ our Lord. *Amen.*

Then shall the Elder say,

O ALMIGHTY God, our Heavenly Father, who of thy great mercy hast promised forgiveness of sins to all them that with hearty repentance and true faith turn unto thee: have mercy upon us; pardon and deliver us from all our sins, confirm and strengthen us in all goodness, and bring us to everlasting, life through Jesus Christ our Lord. *Amen.*

The Collect.

ALMIGHTY God, unto whom all hearts are open, all desires known, and from whom no secrets are hid; cleanse the thoughts of our hearts by the inspiration of thy Holy Spirit, that we may perfectly love thee, and worthily magnify thy holy name, through Jesus Christ our Lord. *Amen.*

Then shall the Elder say,

WE do not presume to come to this thy table, O merciful Lord, trusting in our own righteousness, but in thy manifold and great mercies. We are not worthy so much as to gather up the crumbs under thy table. But thou art the same Lord, whose property is always to have mercy; Grant us, therefore, gracious Lord, so to eat the flesh of thy dear Son Jesus Christ, and to drink His blood, that we may live and grow thereby; and that, being washed through His most precious blood, we may evermore dwell in Him, and He in us. *Amen.*

Then the Elder shall say the prayer of consecration, as followeth:

ALMIGHTY God, our heavenly Father, who of thy tender mercy didst give thine only Son Jesus Christ to suffer death upon the cross for our redemption; who made there, by His oblation of Himself once offered, a full, perfect, and sufficient sacrifice, oblation, and satisfaction for the sins of the whole world; and did institute, and in His holy Gospel command us to continue, a perpetual memory of His precious death until His coming again: hear us, O merciful Father, we most humbly beseech thee, and grant that we, receiving these memorials of the sufferings and death of our Saviour Jesus Christ, may be partakers of His most blessed body and blood; who in the same night that he was betrayed, took bread; (¹) and when He had given thanks, He broke it, and gave it to His disciples, saying, Take, eat; this is my body which is given for you; do this in remembrance of me.

(¹) *Here the Elder may take the plate of bread into his hand.*

Likewise after supper He took (²) the cup; and when he had given thanks, He gave it to them, saying,

(²) *Here he may take the cup in his hand.*

Drink ye all of this; for this is my blood of the New Testament, which is shed for you, and for many, for the remission of sins; do this, as oft as ye shall drink it, in remembrance of me. *Amen.*

Then shall the Minister receive the communion in both kinds, and proceed to deliver the same to the other ministers, (if any be present:) after which, he shall say:

IT is very meet, right, and our bounden duty, that we should at all times, and in all places, give thanks unto thee, O Lord, holy Father, almighty, everlasting God.

Therefore with angels and archangels, and with all the company of heaven, we laud and magnify thy glorious name, evermore praising thee, and saying, Holy, holy, holy Lord God of hosts, heaven and earth are full of thy glory. Glory be to thee, O Lord most high. *Amen.*

THE LORD'S SUPPER. 47

The Minister shall then proceed to administer the communion to the people in order, into their uncovered hands. And when he delivereth the bread, he shall say:

THE body of our Lord Jesus Christ, which was given for *thee*, preserve *thy soul* and *body* unto everlasting life. Take and eat this in remembrance that Christ died for *thee*, and feed on Him in *thy heart* by faith with thanksgiving.

And the Minister that delivereth the cup shall say,

THE blood of our Lord Jesus Christ, which was shed for *thee*, preserve *thy soul* and *body* unto everlasting life. Drink this in remembrance that Christ's blood was shed for *thee*, and be thankful.

[If the consecrated bread or wine be all spent before all have communed, the Elder may consecrate more, by repeating the prayer of consecration.]

[When all have communed, the Minister shall return to the Lord's table, and place upon it what remaineth of the consecrated elements, covering the same with a fair linen cloth.]

Then shall the Elder say the Lord's Prayer; the people kneeling and repeating after him every petition.

OUR Father who art in heaven, hallowed be thy name. Thy kingdom come. Thy will be done in earth as it is in heaven. Give us this day our daily bread; and forgive us our trespasses, as we forgive them that trespass against us; and lead us not into temptation; but deliver us from evil; for thine is the kingdom, and the power, and the glory, forever. *Amen.*

After which shall be said as followeth:

O LORD our heavenly Father, we thy humble servants desire thy Fatherly goodness mercifully to accept this our sacrifice of praise and thanksgiving; most humbly beseeching thee to grant that, by the merits and death of thy Son Jesus Christ, and through faith in His blood, we and thy whole Church may obtain remission of our sins, and all other benefits of His death. And here we offer and present unto thee, O Lord, ourselves, our souls and bodies, to be a reasonable, holy, and lively sacrifice unto thee; humbly beseeching thee that all we who are partakers of this holy communion may be filled with thy grace and heavenly benediction. And although we be unworthy, through our manifold sins, to offer unto thee any sacrifice, yet we beseech thee to accept this our bounden duty and service; not weighing our merits, but pardoning our offenses, through Jesus Christ our Lord: by whom, and with whom, in the unity of the Holy Ghost, all honor and glory be unto thee, O Father Almighty, world without end. *Amen.*

Then shall be said,

GLORY be to God on high, and on earth peace, good-will toward men. We praise thee, we bless thee, we worship thee, we adore thee for thy great glory, O Lord God, heavenly King, God the Father Almighty.

O Lord, the only-begotten Son Jesus Christ; O Lord God, Lamb of God, Son of the Father, that takest away the sins of the world, have mercy upon us. Thou that takest away the sins of the world, have mercy upon us. Thou that takest away the sins of the world, receive our prayer. Thou that sittest at the right hand of God the Father, have mercy upon us. And receive us at last, through the riches of thy grace, into the joy of thine eternal kingdom, where we may reign with thee, world without end. *Amen.*

THE LORD'S SUPPER.

Then the Elder, if he see it expedient, may put up extemporary prayer; and afterward shall let the people depart with this blessing:

MAY the peace of God, which passeth all understanding, keep your hearts and minds in the knowledge and love of God, and of His Son Jesus Christ our Lord; and the blessing of God Almighty, the Father, the Son, and the Holy Ghost, be among you, and remain with you always. *Amen.*

N. B. If the elder be straitened for time, he may omit any part of the service, except the Invitation, the Confession, and the prayer of Consecration.

GENERAL RULES

OF THE

Methodist Episcopal Church.

———◆———

THAT it may the more easily be discerned whether the members of our Societies are indeed working out their own salvation, each society is divided into smaller companies, called classes, according to their respective places of abode. There are about twelve persons in a class, one of whom is styled *the leader*. It is his duty,

I. To see each person in his class once a week at least; in order,

1. To inquire how their souls prosper

2. To advise, reprove, comfort, or exhort, as occasion may require.

3. To receive what they are willing to give toward the relief of the preachers, Church, and poor.

II. To meet the ministers and the stewards of the Society once a week; in order,

1. To inform the minister of any that are sick, or of any that walk disorderly, and will not be reproved.

2. To pay the stewards what they have received of their several classes in the week preceding.

There is only one condition previously required of those who desire admission into these societies—"a desire to flee from the wrath to come, and to be saved from their sins." But wherever this is really fixed in the soul, it will be shown by its fruits. It is, therefore, expected of all who continue therein, that they should continue to evidence their desire of salvation:

First, By doing no harm, by avoiding evil of every kind, especially that which is most generally practiced; such as,

The taking of the name of God in vain.

The profaning the day of the Lord, either by doing ordinary work therein, or by buying or selling.

Drunkenness, buying or selling spirituous liquors, or drinking them, unless in cases of extreme necessity.

Slaveholding; buying or selling slaves.

Fighting, quarreling, brawling, brother *going to law* with brother, returning evil for evil, or railing for railing, the using *many words* in buying or selling.

The *buying or selling goods that have not paid the duty.*

The giving or taking things on usury, i. e., unlawful interest.

Uncharitable or *unprofitable* conversation, particularly speaking evil of magistrates or of ministers.

Doing to others as we would not they should do unto us.

Doing what we know is not for the glory of God: as,

The *putting on of gold and costly apparel.*

GENERAL RULES.

The *taking such diversions* as cannot be used in the name of the Lord Jesus.

The *singing* those *songs*, or *reading* those *books* which do not tend to the knowledge or love of God.

Softness, and needless self-indulgence.

Laying up treasure upon earth.

Borrowing without a probability of paying; or taking up goods without a probability of paying for them.

It is expected of all who continue in these societies, that they should continue to evidence their desire of salvation:

Secondly, By doing good; by being in every kind merciful after their power, as they have opportunity; doing good of every possible sort, and, as far as possible, to all men.

To their bodies, of the ability which God giveth, by giving food to the hungry, by clothing the naked, by visiting or helping them that are sick, or in prison.

To their souls, by instructing, reproving, or exhorting all we have any intercourse with; trampling under foot that enthusiastic doctrine, that "we are not to do good unless *our hearts be free to it.*"

By doing good, especially to them that are of the household of faith, or groaning so to be; employing them preferably to others, buying one of another, helping each other in business; and so much the more because the world will love its own, and them only.

By all possible *diligence* and *frugality*, that the gospel be not blamed.

By running with patience the race which is set before them, *denying themselves, and taking up their cross daily,* submitting to bear the reproach of Christ —to be as the filth and offscouring of the world, and looking that men should say *all manner of evil of them falsely for the Lord's sake.*

It is expected of all who desire to continue in these societies, that they should continue to evidence their desire of salvation :

Thirdly, By attending upon all the ordinances of God; such are,

The public worship of God.

The ministry of the word, either read or expounded.

The Supper of the Lord.

Family and private prayer.

Searching the Scriptures, and

Fasting or abstinence.

www.ingramcontent.com/pod-product-compliance
Lightning Source LLC
Chambersburg PA
CBHW032100220426
43664CB00008B/1083